Take Up Your Cross

DAG HEWARD-MILLS

PARCHMENT HOUSE
LONDON UK

Unless otherwise stated, Scripture quotations are taken from the KING JAMES VERSION of the Bible.

[1]Excerpt in Chapter 2 from *The Trial of J.J.Rawlings* by Kojo Yankah, pages 16-19. Used by permission.

[2]Excerpt in Chapter 3 from *Josephus*, pages 388-389. Used by permission.

[3]Excerpt in Chapter 5 from *Dakes Annotated Reference Bible* page 66. Used by permission.

Published by **Parchment House**

First published 2004

ISBN: 9988-596-15-4

PRINTED IN THE UK

Dedication

To my pastors, **Jacob and Kezia Godwyll**.

God bless you for your courage and sacrifice in becoming the first missionaries to Nigeria.

Contents

CHAPTER 1

Preaching the Cross vs. Preaching Prosperity

Some years ago, I read a book by a well-recognized prophet in which he described an encounter with the Apostle Paul in a vision. I was stunned by the account of his reported interaction with Paul. In this interaction, Paul said to him, *"Except for in a few places in the world, we can hardly recognize the MINISTRY or the MESSAGE that is being preached today."*

He continued, *"When we served, being in the ministry was the greatest sacrifice that one could make and this was reflected in the message of the greatest sacrifice that was made—the cross."*

Some months later, I was walking on a golf course in England with a pastor friend of mine. As we walked and talked, the Lord spoke to me.

He said to me, "Preach about sacrifice."

I said, "Lord, I do not know anything about sacrifice. I have never preached about it." Nevertheless, I had to obey Him. I was surprised to learn so much on this subject and that is why I am writing this book.

I believe in the prophet's vision of the Apostle Paul. I also agree that **the *message* and the *ministry* of the church today are quite different from that of the early church. The concept of sacrificing anything to God is foreign to most Christians today.**

The focus of Christianity today is *MONEY, PROSPERITY, ESTABLISHMENT, SAFETY AND SELF-PRESERVATION.* The goals of most Christians are to get more money, houses, cars, and security. Even pastors measure their success by the amount of money they have, and by the size of the offerings in their churches.

Preaching the Cross vs. Preaching Prosperity

The message of prosperity has become the message of the church.

Church members are postured as receivers—"*Yes Lord, I receive*!" This is the catchphrase of the church! It is time for us to present ourselves before the Lord as people who have something to give.

The church must be seen as a group of people who sacrifice for the Kingdom and not as a group of people who only receive blessings.

You will notice that whenever the church has a miracle convention meeting, the attendance is different from when it is a teaching service, an ordinary weekday service, or a training camp session. Any meeting that calls for some kind of work like witnessing or prayer is poorly attended. However, the crowds gather when they expect to receive miracles. But the church is supposed to be a place where we "take up our crosses and follow Him".

Money has never been a measure of God's approval of our lives and never will be. The Bible clearly teaches that in the last days, some will suppose that gain is godliness.

> **Perverse disputings of men of corrupt minds, and destitute of the truth, supposing that GAIN IS GODLINESS: from such withdraw thyself.**
>
> **1 Timothy 6:5**

"Sacrifice" means "giving up something". It is a central theme of the Bible. Many of us first heard of the word *sacrifice* from the Bible. We read about Abraham's sacrifice, Isaac's sacrifice and Jacob's sacrifice. Throughout the Old Testament, we see the Israelites making sacrifices to God continually. You could not think of a prophet of God in the Bible without thinking about sacrifices. You could not think of Elijah, without thinking of his experience with the 400 prophets of Baal.

Yet, today, *sacrifice* is one of the most hushed topics. Today, the theme of our preaching is prosperity, miracles and blessings. The church has totally abandoned the original message of sacrifice. The church has become a phantom of the original church; fearful and powerless. Other religions constantly demonstrate to us the essence and practice of sacrifice.

The message of sacrifice is very relevant for all of us today. The teaching of sacrifice must return to the church otherwise we will continue to be a phantom of the real church!

Your Heart Follows Your Sacrifice

But lay up for yourselves treasures in heaven, where neither moth nor rust doth corrupt, and where thieves do not break through nor steal: FOR WHERE YOUR TREASURE IS, THERE WILL YOUR HEART BE ALSO.

Matthew 6:20-21

Your heart will be where your treasure is. When I became a pastor, the Lord asked me to put a lot of my own money into the ministry. The Lord made me make many sacrificial donations to help the fledgling church. You see, when you put your money in the church, your heart follows suit.

One of the most painful ways to die is by stoning. Out of the stones thrown, a particular stone will knock you unconscious and kill you. However, before you are hit by the stone that makes you unconscious, all the other stones thrown at you will give you a lot of pain, torture and torment. You suffer a lot from stoning before you actually die.

The Bible tells us that Stephen was stoned to death. As he was dying, his eyes were opened to see Jesus.

But he, being full of the Holy Ghost, looked up steadfastly into heaven, AND SAW THE GLORY

OF GOD, AND JESUS STANDING ON THE RIGHT HAND OF GOD, And said, Behold, I see the heavens opened, and the Son of man standing on the right hand of God.

Acts 7:55-56

How did Stephen see Jesus? I believe he saw Him with the *eyes of his heart*. You see, where your treasure is, that is where your heart will be. When your treasure is in Heaven, your heart is in Heaven. When your heart is in Heaven, the eyes of your heart always see heavenly things.

Let your heart be with God! When your heart is with God, you will be ready to sacrifice; you will be ready to die for what you believe! Not because you have some special calling, but because you believe what you say you believe!

Anything for Christ

But Christ has shown me that what I once thought was valuable is worthless. Nothing is as wonderful as knowing Christ Jesus my Lord. I have given up everything else and count it all as rubbish. All I want is Christ.

Philippians 3:7-8
(Contemporary English Version)

But what things were gain to me, those I counted loss for Christ. Yea doubtless, and I count all things but loss for the excellency of the knowledge of Christ Jesus my Lord: for whom I have suffered the loss of all things, and do count them but dung, that I may win Christ,

Philippians 3:7-8

Paul made many sacrifices for his faith and was glad about it. There is nothing like living for God without paying the price. Jesus said that unless a corn of wheat falls into the ground and dies, it abideth alone. The seed must always die if it is to bear fruit. Some people want to be pastors without paying the price. Be honest with yourself and accept the reality of sacrifice.

In the Foxe's Book of Martyrs, there are several accounts of how people were killed for their faith. They died in droves. Some were eaten by lions.

I would not like to be eaten by a lion. I have been bitten by a lion before and it was not an easy experience. I've seen a lion having lunch before and I certainly wouldn't like to be its supper.

Some of the early Christians were hanged on crosses. Some thought they were not worthy to be crucified in the same way as their master Jesus. So they asked to be crucified upside down.

The Sacrifice Goes on and on

By him therefore let us offer the SACRIFICE of praise to God CONTINUALLY, that is, the fruit of our lips giving thanks to his name.

Hebrews 13:15

I beseech you therefore, brethren, by the mercies of God, that you present your bodies A LIVING SACRIFICE, holy, acceptable unto God which is your reasonable service.

Romans 12:1

In the days of the temple, sacrifices were made to the Lord everyday. It was part of their service and worship to God. It was a daily thing they did for the Lord. There is nothing like a one-time sacrifice that you make for life.

God asks you to present your body as *a living sacrifice*! This type of sacrifice is an undying sacrifice, something that goes on and on. *It is unending!*

One martyr said, "Eighty and four years have I served the Lord. Why should I deny my Lord at this time? What evil has He done to me?" Someone with faith will never deny the Lord!

Furthermore, by these few pages, my son, be admonished because of making many books there is no end.

CHAPTER 2

The Release of Power

For the PREACHING OF THE CROSS is to them that perish foolishness; but unto us which are saved it is the POWER OF GOD.

1 Corinthians 1:18

The cross is the symbol of Christianity. The preaching of the cross is the preaching of sacrifice. It is also the preaching of power. As Christians, we should preach about the cross. In fact, we should have crosses. I have crosses. I have one I keep in my room. *It is the symbol of Christ, the symbol of Christianity and the symbol of the Church!* Some of us think that the fish is the symbol of Christianity. It is not. The cross is that symbol.

I remember meeting one of the politicians in my country. He was one of the most senior ministers of the government and was attending a wedding in our church. After the ceremony he came to my office to meet me. As he sat down, I noticed that he was wearing the emblem of his political party on his lapel. I was amazed at this politician's boldness. He was wearing his party symbol even at a wedding!

Even though his party had become unpopular, he boldly sported this symbol. His party had led the country into difficult times but he was not ashamed of it.

We must be proud of the cross of Jesus Christ. *It is our symbol, and a symbol of obedience and sacrifice*! The Bible tells us in the verse we read, that the preaching of Christ is foolishness to those that are perishing but unto us, it is the power of God.

Sacrifice releases spiritual power! This explains why many demonic rituals involve some kind of sacrifice. Various animals and sometimes human beings are sacrificed in rituals, to release power. Occultists make sacrifices. People seeking spiritual power are always asked to sacrifice something.

The king of Moab sacrificed his son when he saw that he was losing a battle with the Israelites:

> **And when the king of Moab saw that the battle was too sore for him, he took with him seven hundred men that drew swords, to break through even unto the king of Edom: but they could not. THEN HE TOOK HIS ELDEST SON THAT**

SHOULD HAVE REIGNED IN HIS STEAD, AND OFFERED HIM FOR A BURNT OFFERING UPON THE WALL. And there was great indignation against Israel: and they departed from him, and returned to their own land.

2 Kings 3:26-27

This sacrifice turned away the approaching armies. Power was released by sacrificing the king's son. This saved the king's life and the lives of his people. Sacrifice will always release power. Learn this principle-*sacrifice will always release power.*

The Israelites made God angry because they sacrificed their children to idols for power:

Yea, THEY SACRIFICED THEIR SONS AND THEIR DAUGHTERS UNTO DEVILS, And shed innocent blood, even the blood of their sons and of their daughters, whom they sacrificed unto the idols of Canaan: and the land was polluted with blood.

Psalm 106:37-38

Many pastors and leaders of churches are powerless because they make no sacrifices for the Lord and have no intention to do so.

Some years ago, the Church in Switzerland was very powerful. They sent missionaries to Ghana, even though they could not speak Ghanaian languages. One of these missionaries called Johann Riis translated the Bible into Twi, one of the most widely spoken dialects in Ghana. He also translated 6000 Twi proverbs into English.

Today, there are still Swiss people who speak fluent Twi. They are descendants of the original missionaries.

If I were to send people to certain places for missionary work, there would be an outcry. That is why there is no power in our ministries. There is power only when there is sacrifice!

A lot of power is released, for instance, when you fast. This is because a sacrifice is made when you fast. Fasting is sacrificing your meals. When people give up something for the ministry, power is released.

The early church was so powerful. The more they were martyred, the stronger they became. However, when the Church was accepted officially in Rome, it lost its power. This acceptance removed the need for sacrifice and therefore weakened the Church.

The power of the Church is often increased where there is opposition and much need of sacrifice.

Four Types of Power Released through Sacrifice

1. The power to make people follow

There is an aura around anyone who makes great sacrifices. He is respected and held in high esteem by people around him. People see this person doing things that *they* fear to touch. This inspires confidence and stirs up followers to do the same.

The former President of Ghana, Jerry John Rawlings, had many followers. His followers admired and loved him greatly. He was not followed because of his PhDs, or his excellent family background. Paradoxically, he did not have much to boast of in that regard. However, he seemed ready to die for what he believed in.

In May 1979, he attempted a coup d'etat, to overthrow the government of the day. The attempt failed and he was put on trial. But while on trial, he told the court to leave his men alone. He said *he* was responsible for everything that had happened! The bold and sacrificial statements of this young man stirred up the interest and support of many people. Jerry John Rawlings, riding on the wave of this support, became Ghana's head of state and dominated Ghanaian politics for more than twenty years.

It is interesting to read about his trial and what took place afterwards:

> [1]"Mr. President, the principal architect and ringleader in the carrying out of the mutiny is THE FIRST ACCUSED, FLIGHT LIEUTENANT JERRY JOHN RAWLINGS of the Ghana Air Force Station, Accra. He is a young man aged about 31." That was the voice of Director of Public Prosecutions, Mr. G.E.K. Aikins at the opening of the trial

in which six persons had been charged with "Conspiracy to cause Mutiny" and "Mutiny with violence". A seventh accused was facing the charge of "Concealment of Mutiny". The date was Monday, 28 May, 1979. The Burma Hall, conference room of the Ghana Armed Forces, was crowded, following a newspaper report that a court martial was opening that morning. There had been quite a level of anxiety not only in government quarters but also in the military and civilian sectors.

The accused persons were marched in, led confidently by Flt. Lt. J.J. Rawlings who was known to quite a number of soldiers present. He wore dark glasses and was holding something that looked like a scroll sheet. Second accused was Leading Aircraftman John Newton Gatsiko; third accused Leading Aircraftman Sylvanus Tamakloe; fourth accused Cpt. David Baba; fifth accused lanky Leading Aircraftman Albert Kwasi Gbafa; sixth accused Leading Aircraftman Daniel Dzibolosu and the seventh accused was Cpl. Ajowiak Ubald.

Particularly for the hundreds of civilians there, Flt. Lt. J.J. Rawlings was a new face. When he was identified as the first accused, the principal architect of the mutiny, curiosity ran high.

"Mr. President," the prosecutor was addressing the Court Martial, "the first accused had for a long time felt disillusioned about the injustices in our society, more particularly under the Acheampong regime; and so when in

July 1978, the SMC was reconstituted with the removal of Mr. Acheampong as head of state, Jerry John Rawlings thought things were going to improve. When he realized that there were no improvements in the conditions of life, he was struck with dismay and lamented over what he termed 'the tarnished image of the Armed Forces'. He regretted that at the time that the military government was due to hand over to a civilian government, the military government had done nothing to improve the image of the Armed Forces."

The ovation was spontaneous but controlled. The president of the Court Martial was not sure whether it was safe for the proceedings to continue. The general acclaim was that J.J. Rawlings had expressed the true feelings of the junior ranks in the armed forces— what he himself called the conscience of the Armed Forces.

"Mr. President, My Lord Judge Advocate, Members of the General Court Martial, briefly these are the facts upon which these accused persons have been arraigned before you…this state of affairs threw the whole of Accra into a pandemonium during which a number of the civilian population ran helter-skelter and some fat Makola women succeeded in outrunning the thin ones."

The crowd greeted the conclusion of the Prosecutor's statement with laughter—a timely release of the tension that was building up.

As the noise settled, the Judge asked the defense counsel to show up. The team for J.J. Rawlings was Mr. Adumoah-Bossman, but the rest of the accused had not been lucky. However Mr. Adumoah-Bossman pledged that the Bar Association would endeavor to find counsel for the rest.

On resumption, the accused marched back to their seats after consultation with defense counsel. Jerry was heard barking to the rest to 'straighten up and march like soldiers'. Despite the anxiety of the crowd, the six other accused persons didn't have much hope. Some seemed like blaming Jerry Rawlings for all this.

Adjournment was granted for the court to resume in two days.

History did not follow the full text of Jerry's draft speech mentioned by the prosecutor ever to be read. But, in his own handwriting, as obtained from my research, he said:

'Fellow citizens of Ghana,

Now! You listen to me well and good because I am not here to make a speech and I am not here to waste my time talking. First and foremost, I am not here to impose myself on 10 million citizens of this country. But, I am telling you today that I am here today in the history of this country to address myself to military senior officers, all those politicians, all those business men and foreign criminals who have used our blood, sweat and tears—the toils of our laboring—to enrich themselves, to drown in wine and women, while you and I, while the majority of us, are daily struggling for survival, yes!

"I know what it feels like going to bed with a headache for want of food in the stomach.

"Let me give you, the struggling and suffering masses, just one little warning. Should anyone or group of you dare collaborate or help these exploiting pigs to run—this country will once more bleed than we anticipate.

"I am not an expert in Economics and I am not an expert in Law but I am an expert in working on an empty stomach while wondering when and where the next meal will come from.

"I am going to prove to you today it is no longer a question of the military against civilians, it is no longer a question of the Akan against the Ewe, the Ga against the Northerner. But a question of *those who have* against those who *have not*—a question of the vast majority of hungry people against a very tiny minority of greedy, inhuman selfish senior officers, politicians, businessmen and their bank managers and a bunch of cowardly Lebanese who will not stay in their country to fight for a cause. But who is a fool? You and I."

"You and I are the bigger fools for allowing such a blatant abuse of human dignity for so long. 22 years after independence, you and I are still hitting our heads on the ground and leaving it all to God to save us one day. Where on earth has God come to the salvation of a people without the suffering, starving hungry people taking the law into their own hands?

"America has seen her own brand of revolution, France has seen her brand of a revolution. Britain has seen her brand of a revolution. Russia, China, Iran, all of them. Only the black man in the black African Continent goes on leading his fellow black men like a herd of cattle while suppressing them like slaves. Let me tell you today that God will not help you, and the big man will not help you because his stomach is full, his children's stomachs are full and there is enough for them to go and come as they like.

"Only you can help yourselves."

On Wednesday, 30th May, the court martial resumed. There was something very significant this time. On the walls of Burma Camp, leading to the Burma Hall, posters were conspicuous and early arrivals could not miss the message. Some were written in chalk:

"STOP THE TRIAL OR ELSE..."

"IF YOU WANT TO DIE, CONTINUE THIS TRIAL"

"REVOLUTION OR DEATH"

"THE STRUGGLE WILL CONTINUE"

But in no time, the military tore all of them down, just in time for the Court to sit. The front-page banner headlines in the daily newspaper spoke of Jerry fighting against injustices. The statement of the Director of Public Prosecutions was given wide coverage, much to the annoyance of some members of government. That explained the huge uncontrollable crowds that milled in the hall this time.

They cheered openly despite warnings by the Court President, Col J. Enninful. The first witness, Flt. Lt. J.B. Atiemo, confirmed that the first accused had declared that HE WAS PREPARED TO DIE ON BEHALF OF THE REST OF THE ACCUSED. The applause grew wilder.

The next morning, the banner headline of the Daily Graphic read: "LEAVE MY MEN ALONE! I'M RESPONSIBLE FOR EVERYTHING."

The fire caught on. "Here was a real leader," one Corporal Adjei told me later. "In the military, the junior ranks don't like officers who are cowards... moreover, he was saying something all of us had wanted to say a long time ago. WE ONLY NEEDED A LEADER AND WE ALL IDENTIFIED HIM IN FLT. LT. RAWLINGS. EVEN THOSE WHO DID NOT KNOW HIM BEFORE CAME TO LOVE HIM."

The third sitting of the court was on Thursday, 31st May. The defense counsel cross-examined the first prosecution witness amidst shouting and clapping in support of the stand taken by Flt. Lt. Rawlings. Before the President adjourned till Monday, 4th June to enable the Attorney-General's department to find counsel for the other accused persons, he gave what he called a final warning to the public gallery 'to desist from any further shouting and clapping'. He added that he would not hesitate 'to stop the public from listening to the rest of the proceedings'.

The die was cast. As the accused persons were being marched away, SOME OF THE MEMBERS OF THE PUBLIC WAVED AT THEM, SOME WITH FISTS RAISED."[1]

W hen people saw that this 31 year-old man was prepared to die for a cause, it inspired many to follow him. The junior ranks of the army and many civilians rallied to his support. I am not saying that the revolution was right or wrong. All I am showing you is that sacrifice releases the power that makes people follow you.

Let's face it: How many of the democratically elected politicians are prepared to die for what they believe? Some of them do not even believe in their own speeches. They read speeches that are written for them and make promises that are not true. I sometimes marvel at how unreal some of these people are. They rarely speak extemporaneously. Tell me, am I lying?

2. The power to make people believe

Have you ever wondered why some people are so unconvincing? No one wants to hear what they have to say. Have you asked yourself why some pastors have very few members (followers)? Many politicians claim to love their countries. They talk about their concern for their countries at political rallies and news conferences. Unfortunately, many people do not believe them.

Think about Jesus. He never wrote a book and never published an article. He never campaigned for votes or support. In fact, He constantly told people not to publicize the good things He had done for them. He never travelled more than two hundred miles from His hometown. He never preached on TV or on radio. He did not build any institutions to His memory! His picture was never on a billboard and He never owned a car.

Yet, the whole world has gone after Him. Two thousand years have gone by and millions still believe in Him. Thousands are converted to Him daily and there are volunteers who are ready to die for Him today.

What is the reason for the long-lasting effect of His ministry? The answer is simple. The sacrifice! The sacrifice of His life on the cross was the most significant spiritual thing that Jesus did on earth. He preached, He taught and He healed the sick. However, the eternal fruit was borne when He gave up His life on the cross.

Have you ever wondered why Jesus did not stay around longer than 33 years? When He was threatened why didn't He travel to Morocco, Algeria, Macedonia or Egypt? Why didn't He preach for a few more years? Were there no more good works that He could do on earth?

What we need to learn here, is that obedience and sacrifice will bear more eternal fruit than any other good works we do. This one sacrifice for humankind has released so much power into the earth. This is why millions from all nations believe and follow Him. This is why Jesus focused on sacrificing Himself on the cross. The sacrifice on the cross was the key that would release the power of salvation. No amount of preaching or teaching could replace what would be accomplished on the cross.

3. The power to induce commitment

> **But what things were gain to me, those I counted loss for Christ. Yea doubtless, and I count all things but loss for the excellency of the knowledge of Christ Jesus my Lord: for whom I have suffered the loss of all things, and do count them but dung, that I may win Christ,**
>
> **Philippians 3:7-8**

Many great men and women have left all to follow Jesus. Kathryn Kuhlman had to leave her husband. Not many women would be prepared to stay unmarried.

In one of Kathryn Khulman's biographies, the author talks about how he had asked Kathryn about her marriage. He said they were alone in a room together when he asked about this chapter of her life. In a rare moment, she began to speak about her former husband and what it had cost her to leave him.

Suddenly, the power of God entered the office. The writer described how he could hardly stand. He said the presence of God came into the room so powerfully that he had to leave. *A sacrifice always releases power*. Sometimes even talking about the sacrifice releases the power.

I once had an uncanny experience when the holy presence of God walked into my office. I was in conversation with two other pastors when the anointing walked into the room. The three of us suddenly knew that someone had walked in. Everyone there could feel that He was standing by us. These things are real. I had never had an experience like that.

We have more knowledge than we can use, but no sacrifice. There is power ready to break forth in our lives the moment we make the sacrifice. You will be surprised at how many people will become committed to your cause when you make the sacrifice.

4. The power to make people take you seriously

I once asked some pastors, "You preach the same messages that I do, don't you?" Then I asked them, "Is the impact of your message felt?" They stared at me silently.

I continued, "Because you have not given up anything for what you believe, people do not take you seriously. You may say the same things that I do but if you do not pay the price, you will never make the impact you need to."

Many preachers are not taken seriously. Many of their

statements are ignored. But everything changes when someone pays the price. Every situation changes in the moment that blood is shed.

There was a time when our church was attacked. The people in the community were hostile to us. My young men wanted to fight back and kill the invaders. They wanted us to arm ourselves and launch counter-attacks. But I knew that if someone was killed in the confrontation, the intensity and seriousness of the conflict would change forever. This is the reason why we did not fight back when our church was attacked.

Macbeth said , "Blood will have blood!" Jesus said: "He that comes by the sword will go by the sword." The gravity of every situation changes as soon as a sacrifice of someone's life is made. Where there is no sacrifice, there will be no power. You may have many doctrines and ideas, but you will have no power in your ministry. You should come to the Lord and ask Him if there is anything He wants from you. You must give yourself as a living sacrifice to Him. There can be no power without a sacrifice. Sacrifices release the power of God in your life.

When there is sacrifice, there is power. This is why Islamic suicide bombers are making such an impact in the world today. You would think that these terrorist acts would drive people away from their religion. On the contrary, it stirs up more commitment. Sacrifice attracts more followers.

God told me that He called me to start churches. He has asked me to send people to the corners of the world to start churches. The Lord told me that there are several people who will respond to this call. He told me not to worry about people's lives but to sacrifice my best sons and daughters on the harvest fields. I tell you, many have responded and are doing great things for the Lord.

God is going to make you sacrifice. He may change your life and change everything about you. He is going to ask you to give up certain things, and as you do, you are going to see His power. When you speak, your words will be taken seriously because of the sacrifices you've made.

Furthermore, by these few pages, my son, be admonished because of making many books there is no end

CHAPTER 3

The Struggle against the Sacrifice

Since sacrifice releases so much power, the enemies of God have historically fought against the concept of sacrifice. When you make a sacrifice to the Lord, it often looks as though you are doing something stupid. You go down in pain but you come up in victory.

Not surprisingly, the devil has succeeded in keeping believers as far from sacrificing as possible. The Anti-Christ, Pharaoh and Satan himself, all get involved to prevent you from having any such ideas. It is time for Christians to know that power lies just beyond the cross.

Antiochus Epiphanies

And out of one of them came forth a little horn, which waxed exceeding great, toward the south, and toward the east, and toward the pleasant land.

And it waxed great, even to the host of heaven; and it cast down some of the host and of the stars to the ground, and stamped upon them.

Daniel 8:9-10

The Prophet Daniel prophesied about a little horn, which rose to defile the temple. This refers to the reign of Antiochus Epiphanies. He made himself an enemy of the Jews. He profaned the temple, entered the sanctuary, and took away the golden altar. He stopped the daily sacrifice and set up the abomination of desolation upon the altar (an idol), and called Solomon's temple the temple of Jupiter Olympius. This man, a type of Anti-Christ, did not want God's people to sacrifice to their God.

The Anti-Christ

And an host was given him AGAINST THE DAILY SACRIFICE by reason of transgression, and it cast down the truth to the ground; and it practiced, and prospered.

Daniel 8:12

And arms shall stand on his part, and they shall pollute the sanctuary of strength, AND SHALL TAKE AWAY THE DAILY SACRIFICE, and they shall place the abomination that maketh desolate.

Daniel 11:31

Notice right here that, one of the things the Anti-Christ will do is to stop the daily sacrifice. He will stop people from sacrificing to God. Get this clear! The enemies of

God are against you obeying God and laying down your life for Him.

The Anti-Christ will prevail by peace. He will be cast in the mould of Hitler but will be even wiser. He will prosper not by war but by peace. He will win and succeed. He will come in the name of peace; talk about peace, and everybody will think that he is God. But the most significant thing he will do is to stop people from sacrificing to God.

> **And his power shall be mighty, but not by his own power: and he shall destroy wonderfully, and shall prosper, and practise, and shall destroy the mighty and the holy people. And through his policy also he shall cause craft to prosper in his hand; and he shall magnify himself in his heart, and BY PEACE shall destroy many: he shall also stand up against the Prince of princes; but he shall be broken without hand.**
>
> **Daniel 8:24-25**

When the spirit of Anti-Christ is at work, it stops you from sacrificing to God. *Anti-Christ is anti-God and anti-God is anti-sacrifice!* One of the devil's goals is to stop you from sacrificing to God!

The Anti-Christ spirit is against your going to church, giving your money, your time and your life to the work of God. That voice in your life is the voice of the Anti-Christ. The Bible says that the Anti-Christ will come and stop the people from sacrificing to God.

I want you to know that when God is calling on you to

give up something or to do something for Him, *the spirit of the Anti-Christ* will tell you not to do it.

Desolation in Ministry

> **Then I heard one saint speaking, and another saint said unto that certain saint which spake, How long shall be the vision concerning the daily sacrifice, and the TRANSGRESSION OF DESOLATION, to give both the sanctuary and the host to be trodden under foot?**
>
> **Daniel 8:13**

The taking away of the sacrifice is described as the sin of desolation. Desolation means: *destitute, barren, empty, forgotten, dark, rejected and dejected.* The sin of desolation is what comes when sacrifice is taken away from the church.

We cannot build more churches if people are not prepared to sacrifice. People have made sacrifices for us to be Christians today. They made it possible for us to know the Lord. *Where there are no sacrificial people, the church is desolate.*

Our church looked very odd when we sent out missionaries to Africa. It looked as though we were destroying the lives of young promising couples. Parents fought against it with all their might. Yet, these same parents would not mind if the UN gave their children a job in a war zone.

Struggling in the Sun

Recently, I was praying in the presence of God. I was also expecting an important phone call so I had my phone on. (I usually do not have my phone on when I am praying). Then the phone rang. It was one of my lay pastors.

Immediately after speaking to him, I had a vision. I saw the same person walking in a hot desert. He was sweating profusely and struggling in the heat of the shining sun. I knew immediately that he was distressed by his secular job. The Lord showed me that this lay pastor was not where he was supposed to be. So I called him and told him, "Pastor, you are in the wrong place. It is time to give it all up for Jesus. You are called to serve in the house of the Lord. You are a priest."

He responded, "Bishop, it's true, I struggle everyday at work. I know I am lost. I'm coming." That was the end of his secular career. Today he is fruitful in full-time ministry.

It was not easy for me to talk to this lay pastor. I felt very intimidated because he had a good job that was giving him a lot of money. Both Satan and the Anti-Christ were against my talking to this young man about full-time ministry.

Your life will be desolate when you hold back the sacrifice that you must make for God!

May desolation and barrenness be removed from your church and ministry!

Judas Iscariot against Sacrifice

Remember that it was no other person than Judas Iscariot who criticized the woman with the alabaster box. This woman poured out her expensive perfume on Jesus. It was the most valuable thing she had. Women spend hours doing their hair. They know what their hair means to them. A woman's hair symbolizes her beauty. Mary sacrificed her beauty and her valuable things for Jesus.

> **Then took Mary a pound of ointment of spikenard, very costly, and anointed the feet of Jesus, and wiped his feet with her hair: and the house was filled with the odour of the ointment. Then saith one of his disciples, JUDAS ISCARIOT, Simon's son, which should betray him, WHY WAS NOT THIS OINTMENT SOLD FOR THREE HUNDRED PENCE, AND GIVEN TO THE POOR?**
>
> **John 12:3-5**

It is true that this woman had been living in sin. However, she gave what was most precious to her—her hair, her perfume, her tears, to Jesus.

But Judas Iscariot, the honourable treasurer of the team (your treasurer is usually the most trusted person in the organization) didn't like it. Even though it wasn't *his* alabaster box, *his* life or *his* hair that were being sacrificed, he was against it.

The appearances of people who are Anti-Christ or anti-sacrifice, can be very deceptive. The *anti-sacrifice, anti-give-up-everything, anti-do-a-lot, anti-give-a-lot* spirit is the spirit of the Anti-Christ. These people often present themselves as being very decent, very logical, very organized, and dignified. *But it is still the spirit of the Anti-Christ.*

Satan against Sacrifice

From that time forth began Jesus to shew unto his disciples, how that he must go unto Jerusalem, and SUFFER MANY THINGS of the elders and chief priests and scribes, AND BE KILLED, and be raised again the third day. Then Peter took him, and began to rebuke him, saying, Be it far from thee, Lord: this shall not be unto thee. BUT HE TURNED, AND SAID UNTO PETER, GET THEE BEHIND ME, SATAN: thou art an offence unto me: for thou savourest not the things that be of God, but those that be of men.

Matthew 16:21-23

When Jesus explained that He had to die on the cross, one of His pastors, Pastor Peter, took Jesus aside and began to rebuke Him.

"Be it far from you." Pastor Peter said.

"Never! As long as we are here, it will not happen."

Jesus turned and addressed the person who was against His sacrifice and said, "Get thee behind me *Satan*."

Jesus spoke directly to Satan, as the person who was preventing His sacrifice.

We can all understand Peter's love for Jesus. In the natural, the people who love you will often oppose your decision to take up your cross.

Peter did not know that the devil was using him. Our Lord Jesus exposed the devil for who he really was. We all know the story of how Peter rebuked Jesus for suggesting that He would die on the cross. Peter did this in the name of love, care, and concern for his Lord. What he did not know was that, this *love and concern* was actually the *voice of Satan* trying to prevent Jesus from sacrificing Himself.

I qualified as a medical doctor on the 10th of March, 1989. After working for a year, I decided to go into full-time ministry. Many caring relatives were against this idea. My father-in-law was so concerned that he offered to help me get a posting to another medical department. He felt I had lost interest in medicine because I had been posted to the Pathology (dead people's) Department. My dear mother-in-law also was deeply concerned about my situation. She constantly spoke about it.

One day, I said to her, "Please-Teacher (she was a teacher, so all her children called her 'Please-Teacher'), please do not talk about this any more. I have decided to go this way and God will keep me." From that time onwards, she never spoke about my decision to quit practising medicine.

You see, they were concerned about my welfare. Wouldn't you be concerned if your daughter was married to some wild young man who did not want to work any more? Of course, you would be concerned! My mother- in-law loved me just like Peter loved Jesus. *In the natural, this is a sign of great concern. However, in the spirit, it is opposition to the sacrifice.*

The enemy knew that if I sacrificed this treasured and noble profession, power would be released for ministry. All

I was about to do was, to take up my cross and follow Jesus.

To take up your cross does not mean to build a wooden cross and walk to Mount Calvary. It means following the example of Christ Jesus. It means sacrificing your life for Jesus. And truly, much power for ministry has been released since I took that step.

As I write this book, it has been only twelve years of full-time ministry. The Lord has done so much and I am grateful that He called me to this honourable work. Ministry is far more honourable than medicine. In comparison to Christ, everything else is dung.

Satan's Easy Plan

Jesus came into the world to save sinners. In the famous temptation of Christ in the wilderness, Satan showed Jesus the kingdoms of the world.

He said, "I've got a plan. I know your goal is to save the whole world. I have a plan that will avoid pain. This plan will give the same results. There will be no anguish, no torment, and no forfeiting of anything."

Satan continued, "Just bow down and worship me and all these kingdoms will be yours."

But Jesus knew better. He said, "The sacrifice must come on! I have to suffer. I have to die! I have to pay the price!" *Jesus was not fooled by Satan's easy plan.*

Please do not be fooled by Satan's trouble-free plan. There are no shortcuts or easy-jets to the will of God.

Sometimes as pastors, we are nervy when we call on people to make sacrifices. That is the devil at work! I have learnt not to back down. I have learnt to boldly lead people into sacrificing for the Gospel.

Furthermore, by these few pages, my son, be admonished because of making many books there is no end.

CHAPTER 4

Substitute Sacrifice: The Pig in the Temple

And arms shall stand on his part, and they shall pollute the sanctuary of strength, and shall take away the daily sacrifice, AND THEY SHALL PLACE THE ABOMINATION THAT TAKETH DESOLATE.

Daniel 11:31

History shows us that there were people who opposed the offering of sacrifices to God. Not only were they against God's sacrifice but they had a substitute. In place of sacrificing to God, the Anti-Christ will put an "abomination that maketh desolate".

This has happened before. Antiochus made the Jews sacrifice pigs in the temple. These pigs were the substitute for the real sacrifice.

Below is the account of King Antiochus.

King Antiochus: A Type of the Future Anti-Christ

[2]King Antiochus returning out of Egypt, for fear of the Romans, made an expedition against the city of Jerusalem; and when he was there, in the hundred and forty-third year of thc kingdom of the Soloucisdae, he took the city without fighting, those of his own party opening the gates to him. And when he had gotten possession of Jerusalem, he slew many of the opposite party; and when he had plundered it of a great deal of money, he returned to Antioch.

Now it came to pass after two years in the hundred and forty-fifth year, on the twenty-fifth day of that month which is by us called Chasleu, and by the Macedonians Apelleus, in the hundred and fifty-third Olympiad, that the king came up to Jerusalem and pretending peace, he got possession of the city by treachery: at which time he spared not so much as those that admitted him into it, on account of the riches that lay in the temple; but led by his covetous inclination (for he saw there was in it a great deal of gold, and many ornaments that had been dedicated to it of very great value), and in order to plunder wealth, he ventured to break the league he had made.

So he left the temple bare, and took away the golden candlesticks, the golden altar [of incense] and table [of shew bread], and the altar [of burnt offering]; and did not abstain from even the veils which were made of fine linen and scarlet.

He also emptied it of its secret treasure, and left nothing at all remaining; and by this means cast the Jews into great lamentation, for he forbade them to offer those daily sacrifices which they used to offer to God, according to the law.

And when he had pillaged the whole city, some of the inhabitants he slew, and some he carried away captive, together with their wives and children, so that the multitude of those captives that were taken alive amounted to about ten thousand.

He also burnt down the finest buildings, and when he had overthrown the city walls, he built a citadel in the lower part of the city, for the place was high, and overlooked the temple on which account he fortified it with high walls and towers and put into it a garrison of Macedonia.

However, in that citadel dwelt the impious and wicked part of the Jewish multitude. From whom it proved that the citizens suffered many sore calamities. And when the king had built an idol altar upon God's altar he slew swine upon it and so offered a sacrifice neither according to the law, nor Jewish religious worship in that country. He also compelled them to forsake worship which they paid their own God, and to adore those whom he took to be gods and made them build temples and raise idol altars, in every city and village, and offered swine upon them everyday.

He also commanded them not to circumcise their sons, and threatened to punish all that should be found to have transgressed his injunction. He also appointed overseers, who would compel them to do what he commanded.

And indeed many Jews there were who complied with the king's commands, either voluntarily, or out of fear of the penalty that was denounced; but the best men and those of the noblest souls, did not regard him, but did pay a great respect to the customs of their country than concern as to the punishment which he threatened to the disobedient; on which account they everyday underwent great miseries and bitter torment; for they were whipped with rods and their bodies were torn to pieces and were crucified while they were still alive and breathed: they also strangled those women and their sons whom they had circumcised, as the king had appointed, hanging their sons about their necks as they were upon the cross. And if there were any sacred book of the law found, it was destroyed; and those with whom they were found miserably perished also.[2]

There is an important principle here: people who do not sacrifice to God sacrifice to something else! Everybody is sacrificing something. Everybody will sacrifice something. But the question is what will be sacrificed, and to whom will this sacrifice be made?

This has always been God's struggle with His people. The Israelites were constantly worshipping images and sacrificing to idols. They sacrificed even their sons and daughters to other gods and made them pass through fire.

But he walked in the way of the kings of Israel, yea, AND MADE HIS SON TO PASS THROUGH THE FIRE, according to the abominations of the heathen, whom the LORD cast out from before the children of Israel.

2 Kings 16:3

YEA, THEY SACRIFICED THEIR SONS AND THEIR DAUGHTERS UNTO DEVILS, And shed innocent blood, even the blood of their sons and of their daughters, whom they sacrificed unto the idols of Canaan: and the land was polluted with blood.

Psalm 106:37-38

Today, people are not prepared for their sons and daughters to be in ministry. But these same people would love their children to work in risky environments.

In 1 Corinthians 10:20, the Bible declares that the sacrifices the Gentiles make, are made to devils.

But I say, that the things WHICH THE GENTILES SACRIFICE, THEY SACRIFICE TO DEVILS, and not to God: and I would not that ye should have fellowship with devils.

1 Corinthians 10:20

Amon was two and twenty years old when he began to reign, and reigned two years in Jerusalem. But he did that which was evil in the sight of the LORD, as did Manasseh his father: FOR AMON SACRIFICED UNTO ALL THE CARVED IMAGES which Manasseh his father had made, and served them; And humbled not himself before the LORD, as Manasseh his father had humbled himself; but Amon trespassed more and more. And his servants conspired against him, and slew him in his own house.

2 Chronicles 33:21-24

Do not deceive yourself. Sacrifices are made all the time. If you do not do it for one cause, you will do it for another. Sacrifices are made constantly. The Gentiles do make sacrifices but to the devil.

The Sacrifice of Doctors

Medical doctors sacrifice very much for their profession. Medical school lasts seven years and postgraduate medical school lasts another five years.

I recently asked a doctor about how many years he had studied medicine. Amazingly, he had been in medical school for more than twenty years. Is it not amazing! If someone had said he was going to sacrifice two years of his life in a theological school, people would say that he was wasting his time.

If you are in university for twenty years, it means you have a student's income for that long. No one seems to mind a low income for twenty years for the sake of medicine. But a low income for the sake of ministry is not acceptable to most people. Many people would not like to work in a church because they fear they would have a low income.

Near Death Experiences for Christ

I risked my life for medicine, now I risk my life for Christ. I used to sacrifice my "pig in the temple" but now I sacrifice my life to the Lord.

My life has been at risk because of the ministry. There was a time my life was threatened for the ministry. I almost died in a car wreck while on a missionary journey to the north of Ghana. A pastor even said to me, "I wonder why you bother to start churches in such places."

I have almost died in near plane crashes. More than once, I almost died while fasting. It may seem I am involved in a very high risk job.

But what about the risks that doctors take all the time? I remember one night; I was working in the accident centre of Korle Bu Teaching Hospital in Accra, Ghana. I was suturing an accident victim when the needle slipped and accidentally pierced my gloves and finger. My patient's blood and my blood were well and truly mixed together that night. I tell you, I heard the voice of God clearly, "You can die of HIV in disobedience, as you continue to do your own thing."

Doctors are at risk all the time. I know doctors who have contracted the Hepatitis B virus from their work. My pastor in China, who is also a medical doctor, told us that the SARS virus started spreading from the hospital he worked in. He told us that the doctors and other medical staff who had treated the SARS patients had all died.

I could go on to tell you many more risks that doctors take. But no one seems to mind if they die for the cause of medicine. There is a deep disrespect for God and the ministry. It is not seen as something worth dying for.

Dear friend, I would rather die on the mission field than die in the hospital looking after patients.

But I say, THAT THE THINGS WHICH THE GENTILES SACRIFICE, THEY SACRIFICE

TO DEVILS...

I Corinthians 10:20

The Sacrifice of Immigrants

Many people travel to far places and live as second-class citizens in foreign countries. This sacrifice is okay as long as the purpose is to get money. If this were to be done for the sake of missionary work, eyebrows would be raised.

It seems to be acceptable to many. But not for the ministry! I know people who walked across the Sahara Desert to get to Switzerland.

One man told us, "There were three of us who walked through the Sahara Desert. Two of us died and I survived." Is it not amazing that people, who can walk across the Sahara Desert, cannot come to church?

Once in Amsterdam, I was counselling a brother to come to church.

He told me, "I tried four times to come to Europe from Ghana. Four times I stowed away on a ship. Once the captain threw us overboard into shark-infested waters and we swam to the shore."

He said, "When I got to the shore, I found out that I was in Liberia. I went back to Ghana and stowed away again. I did this four times until I finally succeeded in coming to Holland."

He smiled proudly and declared, "I am a Dutch citizen today."

Then I asked, "Why don't you come to church regularly?"

He laughed and mumbled some lame excuse about his work. Surprisingly, this man would not make any effort to be in church but he was prepared to die to be in Holland. This young man risked his life four times to become a Dutch citizen but he wouldn't bother to become a citizen of Heaven.

> **But I say, THAT THE THINGS WHICH THE GENTILES SACRIFICE, THEY SACRIFICE TO DEVILS...**
>
> **1 Corinthians 10:20**

The Sacrifice of Pilots

Pilots and other airline crew make great sacrifices for money. In this era of Osama Bin Laden, terrorism and numerous plane crashes, it is amazing that these people continue to do the work they do. They come up with all kinds of statistics to show that flying is safe.

No one can discount the fear that exists today in airline travel. Nevertheless, there are wives who happily see their pilot-husbands off to the plane and don't think twice about it. These same wives would not allow their husbands to work in the ministry.

What you must see is that the sacrifice to God has been replaced by a "pig in the temple". When you are going on a journey for the Kingdom, you will be asked, "Do you have to go, is it necessary?" Yet, this same sacrifice is done regularly and effortlessly by thousands in the airline industry.

But I say, THAT THE THINGS WHICH THE GENTILES SACRIFICE, THEY SACRIFICE TO DEVILS…

1 Corinthians 10:20

The Sacrifice of Bankers and Accountants

These people spend many hours at work. Some of them come home after nine p.m. every night. They hardly see their families. But this is okay if it is for the bank.

One day, one of my pastors had his mother-in-law visiting. She began to complain about the time that he came home. He reacted, "Mummy, please don't complain about my work. It is because I am in the ministry that you even speak this way."

He reminded his mother-in-law, "What about your son who works at the bank? You know he comes home much later than I do. Yet, you have no complaints about that because you think his work is important enough for him to stay that long."

Unfortunately, the ministry is seen as a second-rate job not worth sacrificing for. "Sacrifice to the devil but don't sacrifice to God!" This is the unspoken message of our friends and relatives.

But I say, THAT THE THINGS WHICH THE GENTILES SACRIFICE, THEY SACRIFICE TO DEVILS…

I Corinthians 10:20

The Sacrifice of Businessmen

Businessmen risk their lives all the time for the sake of money. They travel up and down constantly trying to make deals. Many businessmen come under such pressure and strain that they develop high blood pressure, ulcers and other stress -related diseases. That is the price they pay for acquiring great wealth.

Many businessmen lose their families in the quest for more money. They are hardly at home with their children. They take on the risk of travel and endorse it all in the name of money.

I once heard in the news that all the top executives of St. Louis (a sugar manufacturing company) had perished in a plane crash. This immediately raised the price of sugar.

Do you think top executives do not risk their lives? They do, and sometimes pay a high price for it. People are sacrificing all the time. They will sacrifice their God, their church and their families. They will do anything for more money. They will change their lives, they will live anywhere, and they will travel to obscure places and make all kinds of sacrifices in order to make some more money or achieve their life's goals.

When ministers of the Gospel give themselves to the ministry it is always seen as frivolous and unnecessary. What is more fleeting than the making of money and the building of houses on this earth? We in the ministry have given ourselves to the highest and most worthy calling.

Take a country like Angola. They have had a civil war for more than twenty years. Yet, you will find the British, Americans, and Europeans living there and drilling oil! In the midst of the war in the Democratic Republic of Congo, a Congolese diamond mine was listed on the London Stock Exchange. This means that active business was being conducted in the midst of war. It's amazing what people will do even in the midst of war!

All kinds of British, Dutch and American people are prepared to go to these war-torn African countries and risk their lives if it is for money. They are prepared to go where there is fighting and danger. They are prepared to die for oil, for gold and for diamonds. Nigeria, well known for its dangerous cities and high crime rate is home to many white people who will sacrifice anything for money. In search of more money, British Airways shamelessly flies to Nigeria fourteen times a week.

Yet, were I to ask someone to start a church in certain African countries, the person's family would develop hysteria. There would be all kinds of reasons making me out to be an unreasonable and heartless leader.

This is the point: People are sacrificing, but they are sacrificing to the devil! The sacrifices are being made, but they are being made to the devil. The legitimate sacrifice to God has been replaced by the sacrifice of a pig in the temple.

The Sacrifice for the Dead

Many can give much more for the work of God but they won't. This money would rather be spent on a house, a car or even a funeral.

People attend funerals every weekend in different towns and villages but they can't come to church. I know of someone who spent as much as one thousand pounds sterling to buy the shroud for his mother's funeral. It is not common to see people giving a thousand pounds offering, but people will give it for the dead.

The Sacrifice of Journalists

Reporters and journalists make sacrifices all the time and risk their lives in war zones. Many journalists were killed when America invaded Iraq.

The One-Eyed Journalist

I watched a beautiful one-eyed lady on TV. One eye was covered with a black patch. She was a journalist who had lost her eye while covering a conflict for one of the news networks. As I stared at this one-eyed woman, I marvelled at what people are prepared to do for their jobs. These journalists are honoured for their bravery in covering wars.

Men will honour scientists, doctors, beauty queens, boxers and athletes but they will not honour preachers. God has however promised that when we set our love on Him, He will honour us. I am looking for the honour of God.

Because he hath set his love upon me, therefore will I deliver him: I will set him on high, because he hath known my name. He shall call upon me,

and I will answer him: I will be with him in trouble; I will deliver him, AND HONOR HIM.

Psalm 91:14-15

Seek the honour of God and not the honour of men!

Furthermore, by these few pages, my son, be admonished because of making many books there is no end

CHAPTER 5

Sacrifice: The Master Key to Fruitfulness

And Jesus answered them, saying, The hour is come, that the Son of man should be glorified. Verily, verily, I say unto you, Except a corn of wheat FALL into the ground and DIE, it abideth alone: but if it die, it bringeth forth much FRUIT.

John 12:23-24

This is the missing ingredient. This master key will take the average Christian from barrenness to fruitfulness. Sacrifice is the key that will transform a reverend minister from an official with a title to a truly fruitful minister.

A Readiness to Die

The missing ingredient in some good churches is this—a readiness to die. Many of our churches are going to be small until we have people ready to sacrifice. There comes a time when what is needed is sacrifice. A lot of people have reached the borderline. Many Christians can do more but they don't. It's because they don't want to sacrifice or give up anything.

Not a Lack of Knowledge

Many people do not lack information or knowledge. They know a lot! If you have read my books, you will know a lot of what I know. However, knowledge is not enough! You may not have the fruits that I have even if you have the knowledge that I have. For you to have what I have, you must pay the price. There is a price for everyone to pay. The price of glory is the same for everyone!

This Scripture says that unless a corn of wheat disappears into the ground and dies, it will be alone.

The "corn of wheat" symbolizes the man of God. To be "alone" means "to be fruitless". It means to be without members or followers. The dying process in the man of God will eventually bring out much fruit.

Jesus would not have borne the fruit He did if He had not died on the cross. He would have been alone in Heaven with His Father. He could not have saved us if He had not died and gone to Hell for us. *To win followers for Himself and His Father, He had to fall into the ground and die.*

The corn of wheat has to fall into the ground and die. When the seed falls into the ground, it disintegrates and decomposes. This is what we call "dying". The seed actually goes through a process before it comes out as fruit. That can only take place when it disappears and dies.

This is the most important truth to know. There are many sincere leaders who know many things. They have heard much and think they are high up in God. Knowledge unfortunately breeds pride.

...knowledge puffeth up, but charity edifieth.

1 Corinthians 8:1b

The Kingdom is more than a school of history and doctrines. It is more than acquiring numerous certificates of Bible knowledge. Knowledge without this process will yield nothing. *Have you noticed that some of the most learned and scholarly Bible expositors are very ineffective at real ministry?* In fact, sometimes, the more scholarly they become the more faithless and godless they are.

A single seed will become a big tree with many fruits if it falls into the ground and dies.

There are three processes for the corn of wheat to go through:

1. The Falling
2. The Dying
3. Bearing Fruit.

1. The Falling

The falling into the ground speaks of a period in a man of God's life in which he is unknown and hidden from the view of the general public. It also speaks of a period of rejection, negative response and denial in his life.

Concerning **John the Baptist**, the Bible declares that he was hidden in the wilderness until the time of his showing unto Israel. Every pastor must realize that God has a time when He hides you. Do not be in a hurry to be exposed as premature exposure leads to destruction.

Jesus Christ was hidden for thirty years before He was exposed to public ministry. His appearance in the ministry surprised those who didn't know that a seed had been in the ground for thirty years.

Moses experienced this falling into the ground. He was utterly rejected by his brethren when he first tried to minister to them. He ended up in the wilderness for forty years. After years of rejection and isolation, he was ready to minister.

Joseph had this same experience of falling into the ground. His visions and dreams were utterly rejected. Then he himself was utterly rejected and dispensed with. He found himself first working as a slave and then as a prisoner in Egypt. After several years of separation from his brethren he was finally ready for a great ministry.

These are just a few examples of this pattern of falling into the ground. I tell you, no true minister is truly accepted until he has been first rejected.

I Don't Sow Amongst Thorns

I have experienced this falling into the ground myself. When I started out in ministry, I was utterly and totally rejected by the ministers of the day. One minister that we had a good relationship with, refused to minister to our group any more. When I asked why he wouldn't preach to our group any more, he said, "I don't sow amongst thorns."

He and other pastors claimed I was not called by God and had no business starting a church. They felt I was a medical student who should concentrate on his schooling. They told my assistant not to associate with me because it was dangerous to work with someone who was not called by God.

Which Bible School Did You Attend?

I told another senior minister with whom I had a good relationship, that I had started a church. I simply received a rebuke! Then I was queried as to which Bible school I had attended. Unfortunately, I had not been to Bible school. In discouragement, I went away with my "tail between my legs".

This pastor then decided to hold a campaign right where our church was meeting. He held a big programme and showed a very powerful video of his national and international programmes. It was one of the best presentations of that ministry I had ever seen. Our ministry looked like a group of jokers, dwarfs and midgets together in one place. A powerful invitation to join this great ministry was made that night. After they had left, I asked myself, "Who would want to be with us when there are such powerful and established ministries in the city?"

Are You Mocking Me?

I also remember another incident where I met one of these great pastors of our city. It was at a wedding being held on the university campus.

This pastor and his associate had spoken out against my ministry from their pulpit. They had spoken against people like myself whom they felt were not "called" and therefore should concentrate on medical school. In their eyes, I could never be a pastor!

I went up to him to say hello and he said, "Oh, hello Dag,"

Then he paused, looked at me and said, "Pastor!"

As I stood before him, I felt in my heart that he was mockingly referring to me as a pastor.

I almost asked him, "Sir why are you mocking me? Why do you call me 'pastor' when you don't believe that I am a pastor?"

I don't know how I managed to keep those words from coming out of my mouth. The only thing I felt in that era of my life was rejection.

I went through a period of utter rejection and continued the ministry work in virtual separation from most of the ministers I had known prior to this period.

However, as a result of this separation, God taught me many things.

Don't be worried because you are not accepted or wanted. Don't bother if no one invites you. Your day of showing forth will come. Today, I am even accepted by many who once despised me.

> **And the child grew, and waxed strong in spirit, and was in the deserts till the day of his shewing unto Israel.**
>
> **Luke 1:80**

2. The Dying

When the seed falls to the ground, it disintegrates and decomposes. It utterly changes in its character and appearance. Allow the dying process to occur. Except the seed dies, it abides alone. Unless these qualities that God is going to bring forth in you are allowed to develop, you will never fulfil your ministry.

Two Things that Develop When You Fall into the Ground and Die

1. The development of a personal relationship with God

When men reject you, your relationship with people is minimized. During this period of alienation, you have your best chance to develop a relationship with God. This is the principle that works on people in prison. Their relationship with the outside world is cut off. Many prisoners reflect on the Lord and develop a relationship with God. This is a time where important spiritual traits will be birthed in you. Developing a personal relationship with God is one of the most important things that you will learn when people reject you. Every true minister derives his strength from the Lord directly.

Many will come in that day and say, "I cast out demons in your name and I did great works in your name." But the Lord will say, "I NEVER *KNEW* YOU." "I never knew you," means that I never had a relationship with you. Rejection is sometimes the only way to this all-important relationship.

2. The development of humility

Rejection is a humbling experience. The rejection by man is intended to make you develop humility and humility is the highest mantle a minister can wear. The more humble a minister is, the higher his standing before the Lord is.

One common deception is that the larger your church is, the higher your standing before the Lord. That is not the case. Jesus made it clear that the greatest pastor will be the most humble and childlike amongst us.

> **At the same time came the disciples unto Jesus, saying, Who is the greatest in the kingdom of heaven? And Jesus called a little child unto him, and set him in the midst of them, And said, Verily I say unto you, Except ye be converted, and become as little children, ye shall not enter into the kingdom of heaven. Whosoever therefore shall humble himself as this little child, the same is greatest in the kingdom of heaven.**
>
> **Matthew 18:1-4**

John the Baptist Was Humble

John the Baptist's humility was evident. He made it clear that he was not worthy to unlace the shoes of Jesus. He deferred to the Lord and stated that Jesus must increase and he must decrease. How many pastors today want others to increase while they decrease?

He must increase, but I must decrease.

John 3:30

Jesus Humbled Himself

The humility of Jesus was evident. He humbled Himself and became obedient even to the death of the cross.

And being found in fashion as a man, he humbled himself, and became obedient unto death, even the death of the cross.

Philippians 2:8

Moses Was Humbled

Moses lost all confidence in himself. The Bible calls him the meekest man on earth. Wouldn't you be meek after forty years in the wilderness as one of the ten most wanted men in Egypt? When you read about the call of Moses, you see how Moses had zero confidence in himself. He was a great man but his opinion of himself was genuinely very low because he had suffered rejection. Notice the low esteem that Moses had of himself.

[3]The Ten Complaints of Moses

1. And Moses said unto God...**Who am I**? Exodus. 3:11
2. And Moses said unto God…**what shall I say unto them**? Exodus 3:13
3. And Moses answered…**they will not believe me**… Exodus. 4:1
4. And Moses said…**I am not eloquent...I am slow of**

speech, and of a slow tongue. Exodus 4:10

5. And he said, **O my Lord, send, I pray thee, by the hand of him whom thou wilt send.** Exodus 4:13
6. And Moses...said, **Lord...why is it that thou hast sent me?** Exodus 5:22
7. And Moses spake...**the children of Israel have not hearkened unto me**...Exodus 6:12
8. And Moses said...**I am of uncircumcised lips**...Exodus 6:30
9. And Moses cried unto the LORD...**they be almost ready to stone me**. Exodus 17:4
10. And Moses said unto the LORD, **Wherefore hast thou afflicted thy servant?**... Numbers 11:11

Joseph Was Humbled

Joseph, after being a prisoner for some years did not think of vengeance when he saw his brothers. He could see through it all, that God had meant it for good.

> **Now therefore be not grieved, nor angry with yourselves, that ye sold me hither: for God did send me before you to preserve life. So now it was not you that sent me hither, but God...**
>
> **Genesis 45:5,8**

Joseph had so matured in the things of God that he felt his brothers had done nothing wrong. In fact, he felt his brothers were used of God.

I've Been There

After going through all that I have been through, I have come to love and appreciate the people who once rejected me. I feel that God used them to train me in the ministry. I bear none of them a grudge and I value their ministries greatly. Even the bitterest of experiences have worked out for my good.

3. Bearing Fruit

Bearing fruit is a very spiritual thing. Most men of God think that if you have a large church, you have borne much fruit and are pleasing to the Lord.

However, you will notice that Jesus was pleasing to His Father even before He preached His first sermon. He pleased God long before He was publicly known. You can please God even when you are not famous.

> **And lo a voice from heaven, saying, This is my beloved Son, in whom I am well pleased.**
>
> **Matthew 3:17**

You don't have to have a church for the Heavenly Father to say: "This is my beloved son in whom I am well pleased." You don't even have to be a pastor. You don't have to write a book. You don't have to preach a sermon to hear the words, "This is my beloved son in whom I am well pleased."

You don't need to be famous to hear the words, "This is my beloved son in whom I am well pleased." Jesus was not famous when this happened. This Scripture shows us that pleasing God is not based on our works per se. Any fruits we bear are actually gifts that are given by the Lord.

Have you wondered at the immense fruit that Christ Jesus bore? Two thousand years have gone by and He has more fruit than He has ever had before. What did He do that brought about so much fruit?

He did six things: three years of preaching, teaching and healing, His humility, obedience and the sacrifice on the cross. Significant among these things was His sacrifice on the cross which opened the door for our salvation. By far, the greatest thing that Christ did for us was to die on the cross for our sins. Jesus finally bore much fruit after His sacrifice.

Furthermore, by these few pages, my son, be admonished because of making many books there is no end

CHAPTER 6

How to Come Close to the Anointing

Old Testament Sacrifices Are an Example for Us Today

In the Bible times, you could not even think of worshipping God without making a sacrifice. You simply had not worshipped God until a sacrifice was made.

Poor people sacrificed little birds like pigeons and turtledoves. They could not afford to bring sheep, goats and cows. You were required to sacrifice whatever you had. *But there had to be some sacrifice!* Can we say we worship God, if we present no sacrifice?

You may say, "Christ has sacrificed for us. No further sacrifices are needed." No one is asking you to die on the cross again! Nevertheless, Jesus told us to *take up our crosses and follow Him*, didn't He? This means that even though Christ has made the ultimate sacrifice, we are still to follow His example of self-sacrifice.

There are lessons to be learnt from the Old Testament system of sacrifices. The Old Testament is a treasure house of teaching for New Testament Christians.

Do You Know How to Use the Old Testament?

Anyone who doubts that the Old Testament is very relevant today should just read on. The following are a number of reasons why Old Testament Scriptures are useful today:

a. **Christ Himself expounded the things in the Old Testament Scriptures concerning Himself in the Law, the Psalms, and the Prophets.**

> **Ought not Christ to have suffered these things, and to enter into his glory? And beginning at Moses and all the prophets, he expounded unto them in all the scriptures the things concerning himself. And he said unto them, These are the words which I spake unto you, while I was yet with you, that all things must be fulfilled, which were written in the law of Moses, and in the prophets, and in the psalms, concerning me. Then opened he their understanding, that they might understand the scriptures,**
>
> Luke 24:26-27, 44-45

b. **The things that were written aforetime in the Old Testament Scriptures were written for our learning, that we through patience and comfort of the Scriptures might have hope.**

For whatsoever things were written aforetime were written for our learning, that we through patience and comfort of the scriptures might have hope.

Romans 15:4

c. Jesus Himself came to fulfil the Law and the Prophets.

Think not that I am come to destroy the law, or the prophets: I am not come to destroy, but to fulfil. For verily I say unto you, Till heaven and earth pass, one jot or one tittle shall in no wise pass from the law, till all be fulfilled.

Matthew 5:17-18

d. Jesus said that the Law and the Prophets prophesied.

For all the prophets and the law prophesied until John.

Matthew 11:13

e. The Old Testament prophets spoke of the sufferings of Christ and the glory that should follow. It was revealed to them that their utterances did not just concern their own generation but another.

Of which salvation the prophets have inquired and searched diligently, who prophesied of the grace that should come unto you: Searching what, or what manner of time the Spirit of Christ which was in them did signify, when it testified before-

hand the sufferings of Christ, and the glory that should follow. Unto whom it was revealed, that not unto themselves, but unto us they did minister the things, which are now reported unto you by them that have preached the gospel unto you with the Holy Ghost sent down from heaven; which things the angels desire to look into.

1 Peter 1:10-12

f. **The things, which happened in Old Testament history in Israel, were for types and examples and these things are written for our admonition upon whom the ends of the ages are come.**

Now these things were our examples, to the intent we should not lust after evil things, as they also lusted. Now all these things happened unto them for ensamples: and they are written for our admonition, upon whom the ends of the world are come.

1 Corinthians 10:6,11

g. **The writer of the book of Hebrews said, "In the volume of the book it is written of Me," that is, of Christ.**

Then said I, Lo, I come (in the volume of the book it is written of me,) to do thy will, O God.

Hebrews 10:7

Sacrifice and offering thou didst not desire; mine ears hast thou opened: burnt offering and sin offering hast thou not required. Then said I, Lo, I

come: in the volume of the book it is written of me, I delight to do thy will, O my God: yea, thy law is within my heart.

Psalm 40:6-8

h. **The Scripture speaks of, "first the natural and afterwards that which is spiritual", and this is a principle which may well be applied in this study.**

Howbeit that was not first which is spiritual, but that which is natural; and afterward that which is spiritual. The first man is of the earth, earthy: the second man is the Lord from heaven.

1 Corinthians 15:46-47

All these points I have enumerated show us that the Old Testament can and must be used as sound teaching material. We cannot afford to ignore the revelation that is contained in the Old Testament.

How Close to the Anointing Do You Want to Be?

A study of the tabernacle of Moses reveals that there was always the pain of sacrifice before the priest could approach the holy presence of God. The sacrifice had to be made at the door of the tabernacle.

This position of the altar of sacrifice (at the door) signifies that there is the need to *first* offer a sacrifice if you want to go deeper into the things of God.

The Holy of Holies, the place of anointing, was the innermost room in the tabernacle. Without walking through the place of sacrifice, you could not come to this place of anointing. How close do you want to be to the innermost room? How near do you want to be to the anointing? This is an important lesson to all of us.

I do not know of any great man of God who climbed to great heights in ministry without paying the high price of sacrifice. Many people know the Scriptures and the doctrines, but are not prepared to pay the price of ministry. Therefore, they remain powerless and empty-handed in the face of a lost and dying world.

> **And THOU SHALT KILL THE BULLOCK BEFORE THE LORD, BY THE DOOR of the tabernacle of the congregation.**
>
> **Exodus 29:11**

The wave offerings and the heave offerings were needed to bring you closer to God. This is why we need to bring sacrifices to the house of the Lord. As we make sacrifices, we get nearer and nearer to the inner room (place of anointing). We are brought near to the anointing by the blood. It is the blood and the sacrifice that enables us to come near to the anointing!

> **But now in Christ Jesus ye who sometimes were far off ARE MADE NIGH BY THE BLOOD (sacrifice) of Christ.**
>
> **Ephesians 2:13**

Furthermore, by these few pages, my son, be admonished because of making many books there is no end.

CHAPTER 7

The Elimination of Pharaoh

Pharaoh is a biblical model or type of Satan. This is because he keeps the people of God in bondage and refuses to let them go. Pharaoh struggled with the children of Israel until they finally got out of Egypt and were on their way to the Promised Land. Even then he did not give up. He was bent on recapturing the Israelites.

Satan will do almost anything to keep you in bondage. He chased the people of God until the Lord eliminated the Egyptians finally and permanently. The Lord stopped Pharaoh and his influence on the children of Israel.

How will Pharaoh finally be eliminated from your life? What will break satanic strongholds in your life? All you have to do is to follow the example of the Israelites and you will be free forever.

This chapter talks about the elimination of Satan and his demonic chains from your life and ministry.

Walking through the Red Sea

"Walking through the Red Sea" symbolizes walking into almost certain death. It signifies walking away from safety into a realm where you can only trust God. In the New Testament, walking through the Red Sea stands for the dying process.

Sometimes, walking by faith appears as though you are being led into your own destruction. Walking through the Red Sea is a powerful tool that God uses to eliminate enemies. Walking through the Red Sea is an action in which you rely on God's grace.

When you walk through the Red Sea, you do not depend on money, friends, family, or natural forms of assistance.

Pharaoh Could Not Go Through the Red Sea

Satan can chase you and harass you. But there are certain places he cannot go to.

The devil is not all-knowing and all-powerful. To escape from Pharaoh and his agents you need to go where he cannot follow. When you sacrifice to the Lord, you go through the Red Sea. This is because you walk through a dying and a losing process.

When you walk through the Red Sea, you sacrifice your future and place yourself in the hands of God. I am sure you know that it is not a normal thing to walk through the seabed with a wall of water to your right and a wall of water to your left. What if you get stuck in the middle? What if the water comes tumbling down?

> **Speak unto the children of Israel, that they turn and encamp before Pi-hahiroth, between Migdol and the sea, over against Baal-zephon: before it shall ye encamp by the sea. For Pharaoh will say of the children of Israel, They are entangled in the land, the wilderness hath shut them in. And I will harden Pharaoh's heart, THAT HE SHALL FOLLOW AFTER THEM; and I will be honoured upon Pharaoh, and upon all his host; that the Egyptians may know that I am the LORD. And they did so.**
>
> **Exodus 14:2-4**

Pharaoh's (Satan's) aim is to keep you from Christ. Pharaoh failed in his attempt to keep the people from knowing their God. However, Pharaoh does not give up easily. He says, "Chase him, and track him down. Prevent him from going too far."

The devil aims at keeping you from the ministry. Have you wondered why you have undergone such a struggle since you decided to serve the Lord? It is because Pharaoh is chasing hard on your heels.

The Baptism of Death

Paul teaches us that going through the sea was a baptism for the children of Israel. It was a symbolic baptism. They entered into the depths of the sea and came out again.

Moreover, brethren, I would not that ye should be ignorant, how that all our fathers were under the cloud, AND ALL PASSED THROUGH THE SEA; AND WERE ALL BAPTIZED UNTO MOSES IN THE CLOUD AND IN THE SEA;

1 Corinthians 10:1-2

You can compare this to what the Bible says elsewhere:

Know ye not, that so many of us as were baptized into Jesus Christ were baptized into his death? Therefore we are buried with him BY BAPTISM INTO DEATH: that like as Christ was raised up from the dead by the glory of the Father, even so we also should walk in newness of life.

Romans 6:3-4

By baptism, we are symbolically buried with Jesus. Baptism is therefore a symbol of sacrifice and death.

When you walk through the Red Sea you eliminate Pharaoh and his agents. When you die to yourself, your desires, your needs and your wants, you eliminate Pharaoh and all other enemies.

This is how the children of Israel got rid of their enemies: by sacrificing their lives in the Red Sea. God began to fight for the Israelites *only* when they entered into the Red Sea.

When we're not afraid to sacrifice ourselves and walk into the Red Sea; when we allow ourselves to die in Christ, our enemies perish behind us!

If the Israelites had stayed out because of fear, Pharaoh would have recaptured them. They would have been killed in the desert. *Many people die of the things they fear. The things that many of us are afraid of eventually happen.* Death in the Red Sea is better than being killed in the desert.

Discussion by the Red Sea

I have observed people who have shied away from full-time ministry. Mostly, people stay away from the ministry because of the fear of poverty and ridicule. They fear that they will perish in the Red Sea.

I have watched these same people stand at the shore of the Red Sea and discuss how they intend to eventually, one day, go through this sea. They say things like, "Oh, that is my ultimate goal. As for full-time ministry, I know that I will by all means do it." They carry on, "By all means, I will get to that point. I know in my heart that is what I want to do one day."

They explain, "We all get to that point at different times."

Then I have watched Pharaoh descend upon these people. Suddenly, their lives become one long battle as they try to ward off Pharaoh and the world's system. Soon these people who were just about to go through the Red Sea don't have time to even go to church. They are fully entangled with Satan and the world's system.

As the battle continues at the shores of the Red Sea, negotiations with Pharaoh start. Soon, a compromise is reached, so that an individual is never to consider going through the Red Sea. I have watched this happen many times. Today, I know people who would have been fruitful ministers of God if they had made the sacrifice much earlier. Are you stuck on the shores of the Red Sea?

I Can't Believe He Is Going Through

When you give your precious life to God, you walk through the Red Sea. When you give your future to God, you walk through the Red Sea.

The enemy stands at the shores of the sea and says, "I can't believe he's going in!! I can't believe he's giving up his life. I tried to frighten him about the dangers of the Red Sea ministry." The devil knows that he can't follow you through your sacrifice. Satan remembers how he perished when he tried to follow Moses.

He laments: "I can't believe it! I've had this experience before! I remember what happened to me at the Red Sea and I do not want to go into the sea again." *(The devil will lose his control over you when you give up everything for God).*

It is true. He will lose his control. The devil does not lose his control because of the message you heard. He does not go away after we anoint you with oil, and pray for you.

Until you go through the Red Sea, the world still has control. As long as you stand there and refuse to enter, Pharaoh has access to you! As long as you refuse to die and give up what you're supposed to give up, the world's system will dominate you.

Pharaoh, Dirty Daniel and Freaky Freda

A beautiful young lady became born again. She had had several boyfriends in the past. Slappy Jay, Ricky Zee,

Kweku Killer, Big Bobo were all part of the squadron. Zee! Her current and steady lover whom she was planning to marry was none other than the swanky toe-tapping, cool-rapping Dirty Daniel, a favourite with the ladies. Zig zag!*

However, one day, she attended a breakfast meeting and gave her life to Christ. To say the least, Pharaoh was very angry at the loss of one of his slaves.

For a few months, Pharaoh thought this young lady would return to Egypt. But her commitment to the things of God grew. At an emergency session, Pharaoh decided to get her back at all costs or to kill her.

Pharaoh hatched up a plan to kill Freaky Freda with HIV. Pharaoh knew that Freaky Freda could not resist Dirty Daniel.

One night, Satan ensured that Dirty Daniel was fully loaded with HIV from his other girlfriend, Slippery Susie.

Pharaoh smiled confidently as he charged Dirty Daniel to infect and destroy Freaky Freda for her unfaithfulness to him.

Dirty Daniel called Freaky Freda, "Hi baby, I miss you baby."

He continued, "Where have you been? I've been calling your number all weekend. The answer was always the same, "The mobile number you have dialled is either switched off or out of coverage area."

"Oh, I was at a camp meeting," she answered.

"Camp meeting," he retorted. "What on earth is that?"

"It is a meeting for Christian leaders in my new church," she informed him.

"Oh, I see. Anyway, I miss you. Do you miss me? Can I come to your place tonight?"

"Yes, I've wanted to see you myself. There is something I need to tell you," she answered. "I'll be home early."

Pharaoh and his legions began rejoicing in advance. "The plan is working, we will end this rebellion."

But that night, Dirty Daniel had the shock of his life.

Freaky Freda said, "No! I am sorry I cannot continue this relationship with you."

"Don't you love me?" he asked. "Don't you want to marry me?"

She told him tearfully, "It's not been easy for me, I've been crying all day. But I have decided to sacrifice this relationship so that I can serve the Lord."

In the moment that Freaky Freda sacrificed her relationship with Dirty Daniel, *she walked through the Red Sea and went out of the reach of Pharaoh.*

Pharaoh and legions stood by the shore in shock. They said, "We can't believe she's going in!! We can't believe she's doing it! We are losing control over Freaky Freda."

The devil knows that he can't follow you through your sacrifice. As you sacrifice your profession for the Lord, Satan loses his influence over your life.

Furthermore, by these few pages, my son, be admonished because of making many books there is no end.

**The expressions "merzee, zee, zaa, zimbo, zig zag" are author's colloquial exclamations.*

CHAPTER 8

Let Him Deny Himself

Then said Jesus unto his disciples, If any man will come after me, LET HIM DENY HIMSELF, and take up his cross, and follow me.

Matthew 16:24

And HE THAT TAKETH NOT HIS CROSS, and followeth after me, is not worthy of me.

Matthew 10:38

My Journey with the Cross

The phrase "if any man" defines those who must take up the cross. Self-denial is one of the basic truths of the Gospel. I do not know of any stronger statement that our Lord made. In this Scripture, He defines those who cannot be His disciples. This act of taking up your cross, clearly draws a line between those who qualify and those who do not.

Those who therefore cannot be Christians are those who are not prepared to deny themselves. Where are crosses usually taken to? To restaurants, parties, or weddings? No sir! Crosses are carried to the place of execution and suffering. This Scripture has only one meaning: it means that we must follow the example of Jesus Christ and lay down our lives in obedience to Him. Are you obeying the Lord?

I got to know the Lord at about the age of fifteen. I have constantly had to take up my cross, deny myself and follow the Lord. Without doing this, my Christianity would always have been a phantom of what true Christianity is supposed to be. Dear friend, Christianity then and now is not easy.

The Music I Used to Listen to!!

During my early years as a Christian, I learned to say "no" to things which ordinary people said "yes" to. One of the first things I had to deny myself of was **non-Christian music.** I used to love music by Lionel Richie, Michael Jackson, the Bee Gees and ABBA. The key verse that guided me in those days was 1 Corinthians 10:23: "All things are lawful but not all things are helpful."

> **All things are lawful for me, but all things are not expedient: all things are lawful for me, but all things edify not.**
>
> **1 Corinthians 10:23**

I really loved and still do love music, but there was no way I was going to continue my walk with Christ and listen to that kind of music. Although nice to the ear, it is not spiritually helpful.

There are many Christians who don't do well because they are not prepared to deny themselves of certain worldly things.

The Places I Used to Go to!!

There were **places** I used to go to that I had to stop going to if I was to continue with the Lord. Dear friend, you cannot go to the same old places. Except you deny yourself, you cannot be a Christian. I used to go a-gambling at the racecourse every Saturday. I was an avid horse lover and a regular patron of the racecourse. When I got saved, I had to deny myself the pleasure and foolishness of gambling.

The Friends I Used to Have!!

Even as I write this book, I realize how essential it is for Christians to deny themselves of many things if they want to serve the Lord. I had a set of friends before I got saved. When I got saved, I realized that these unbelieving friends would not be helpful.

The Job I Used to Do!!

There are times you have to give up certain jobs in order to serve the Lord.

I remember a brother whom I led to the Lord. I saw him saying the sinner's prayer. A few days later, I prayed for him to receive the Holy Spirit baptism. I personally laid hands on him and watched him receive the Holy Ghost baptism and saw him speak in tongues. I also counselled him about his lifestyle.

I told him, "You have to change your lifestyle. You have to say "no" to the old things, old people and old places of your life." One day, I noticed that this brother had stopped coming to church regularly.

I asked him, "What is happening?"

He told me, "I have a new job at such and such hotel."

He continued, "We work in the night and at weekends."

Then I probed further, "What exactly do you do at this hotel?"

He mumbled some feeble answer, and I could tell immediately that it was not a decent job. Night after night, he worked amongst smoking, drinking and rollicking men and women of sin, as they danced their lives away on the floor of the nightclub.

This was no atmosphere for a good Christian. It was only a matter of time, before my friend completely backslid. The next time I saw him, he was deep in the world and high on drugs.

The Business I Used to Run!!

You see, except you deny yourself, you cannot be a disciple of Christ. I remember another church member, who owned a restaurant in a hotel. One day, in a move to expand the business, the hotel granted him use of a nightclub facility. When I visited the premises, I wondered to myself, "What in the world is a Christian going to do with such a space?"

He said, "Oh, they will just play music in the evenings." This "music in the evenings" degenerated into a nightclub environment with half-dressed girls singing every night. I thought to myself, "How long will this Christian brother be able to stay in the faith?" To cut a long story short, the last I heard of him, he was out of the church and fully established in the world.

He had fallen into any kind of dark sin that you can think of. I also heard that he was in a mental hospital.

There are times you will have to sacrifice your job so that you can follow Christ. Not all jobs are from the Lord. Every good and perfect gift comes from the Lord.

The Films I Used to Watch!!

The films I used to watch, I could watch them no more. That was not easy for me because I really enjoyed watching films. It is not everything we watch that pleases the Lord. I would go to different cinema houses in my city and have a good time watching all kinds of films.

One day, I was watching a Chinese film at Orion Cinema in Accra, Ghana. I thought it was a safe film. Suddenly, the hero of the film developed a fever. As he lay shivering under his blanket, it was decided that the only thing that could cure his fever and keep him warm was a group of naked girls. This film had suddenly changed in its character. That was a turning point for me. I decided to deny myself of this as well. These things may seem trivial to you, but it is the failure to deny yourself these very things that prevents us from walking with God.

As I walked with the Lord, I continually had to deny myself of many other things. One of the things I had to deny myself of was useless socializing. I also learnt how to deny myself of food so that I could fast. As you can see, little by little, and step by step, you take up your cross, deny yourself and follow Jesus.

Furthermore, by these few pages, my son, be admonished because of making many books there is no end.

CHAPTER 9

Take Your Room in Ministry

...and Elisha the son of Shaphat of Abel-Meholah shalt thou anoint to be prophet IN THY ROOM.

1 Kings 19:16

God has called many of us. However, you have to pay the price in order to take your place in the ministry. Your place in the ministry is also called your "room" of ministry. Everybody has a room or position that he occupies in ministry. This room of ministry defines your standing before God. It also identifies and classifies you among the ranks of God's numerous servants.

It requires something to occupy that room. You need to pay the price to occupy that place. The gift or the sacrifice is what will make room for you.

A man's gift MAKETH ROOM FOR HIM, and bringeth him before great men.

Proverbs 18:16

One day, when you get to Heaven, you will either have a room waiting or not. This will depend on your obedience to the Lord. The gift you give creates a space, and makes room for you.

I occupy a particular spiritual position in my country. At the spiritual gates of the country and among the spiritual elders, I occupy a particular chair. It may not be a very great position but it is a position anyway. That is the room God has given me.

Perhaps, God has given you a place in the ministry. God has prepared a place for you among the ranks of the ministers. Do you *want* that place? Do you *like* that place? Will you take your place or will someone else have to take it?

You Can Be Replaced

Even while in your room of ministry, you can be replaced by someone else. Elisha was given Elijah's room of ministry. He complained about the ministry. He felt he had sacrificed so much for the Lord. He erroneously thought that he was the only one doing something for the Lord. God told him, "There are seven thousand pastors and churches you don't know about."

> **And it was so, when Elijah heard it, that he wrapped his face in his mantle, and went out, and stood in the entering in of the cave. And, behold, there came a voice unto him, and said, What doest thou here, Elijah? And he said, I have been very jealous for the LORD God of hosts: because the children of Israel have forsaken thy covenant, thrown down thine altars, and slain thy prophets with the sword; and I,**

even I only, am left; and they seek my life, to take it away. And the LORD said unto him, Go, return on thy way to the wilderness of Damascus: and when thou comest, anoint Hazael to be king over Syria: And Jehu the son of Nimshi shalt thou anoint to be king over Israel: and Elisha the son of Shaphat of Abel-meholah shalt thou anoint to be prophet in thy room. And it shall come to pass, that him that escapeth the sword of Hazael shall Jehu slay: and him that escapeth from the sword of Jehu shall Elisha slay. Yet I have left me seven thousand in Israel, all the knees which have not bowed unto Baal, and every mouth which hath not kissed him.

1 Kings 19:13-18

Many years ago, I had a strange vision. In the vision, I saw a man sitting on a chair. I did not know who the man was. Suddenly, a hand appeared and this hand picked the man by his collar and lifted him out of his chair. The hand then lifted me by my collar and placed me in that chair. The Lord revealed to me that I was replacing someone. He said to me that I was to occupy a chair that someone else had occupied before.

There are many reasons why God may replace you. You can be replaced if you do not sacrifice to take your room. There is a place among the Christian heroes for you.

I've known people who failed to stand in the room that God gave them. It wasn't long before somebody else took up that room. If you fail to take the step when you should, others will be brought in to replace you.

Are You Worthy of the Room?

Jesus was placed in a position of honour. He is the only one who sits at the right hand of God the Father. He was the one who was allowed to open and to read the book. He was found worthy to do these things because He is the "lamb that was slain". "Thou art worthy to take the book and to open the seals *because* thou art the lamb *that was slain*."

> **And I wept much, because NO MAN WAS FOUND WORTHY to open and to read the book, neither to look thereon. And one of the elders saith unto me, Weep not: behold, the Lion of the tribe of Juda, the Root of David, hath prevailed to open the book, and to loose the seven seals thereof. And I beheld, and, lo, in the midst of the throne and of the four beasts, and in the midst of the elders, stood a Lamb as it had been slain, having seven horns and seven eyes, which are the seven Spirits of God sent forth into all the earth. And he came and took the book out of the right hand of him that sat upon the throne. And when he had taken the book, the four beasts and four and twenty elders fell down before the Lamb, having every one of them harps, and golden vials full of odors, which are the prayers of saints. And they sung a new song, saying, THOU ART WORTHY TO TAKE THE BOOK, and to open the seals thereof: for thou wast slain, and hast redeemed us to God by thy blood out of every kindred, and tongue, and people, and nation;**
>
> **Revelation 5:4-9**

The Famous Evangelist

When you listen to an evangelist preaching, you may think that you could preach better than he does. You could probably preach circles around him. However, that does not qualify you to stand in *his room* of ministry. You may actually know more than he does and have a better character than he does. Nevertheless, it is God who gives the room to the minister. There are questions and speculations about many successful ministers. Many wonder why such people are so successful. Why does anyone listen to this person? Why does anyone come for his crusades?

This person is occupying a room of ministry given to him by the Lord. One day, as I observed a famous evangelist preach at a crusade, I thought to myself, "I could probably preach this message better." I marvelled that so many thousands had gathered to hear such a message.

When it was time to pray for miracles, there were hardly any healings. Yet the crowds kept coming, night after night. As I mused over this, I knew that if this were my crusade, no one would attend to hear my "good preaching".

The Lord spoke to me and said, "I have given this man of God a room. He occupies a position that he did not create for himself. He has paid a price to be in that room. It is not by his preaching, organization or even healings, but by the room that I have placed him in."

What Have You Been Through?

I once formed an association of pastors.

One senior minister asked me, "What do you think

you're doing? Do you know what it means to form an association of churches and pastors?" Then he asked me a question: "What have you been through, what have you suffered, what have you survived?" What he was asking was, "Have you paid the price to be the leader of an association of churches and pastors?"

He continued, "I have contended with the prince of this nation. What have *you* been through, what have *you* suffered, what have *you* survived?" Later on, I discussed with this pastor about how the government was persecuting me. He already knew about how the government of the day had broken our walls and attacked us in the night.

But I told him, "That is not all. After breaking our walls, they sent the Internal Revenue Service to hound us. All my pastors came under investigation. Then they turned their attention on me personally."

I had to fill various forms and I was interrogated at their offices. They questioned me extensively and wanted to know about my car, home, money etc. I sent my Chief Accountant but they refused to see him. They insisted that I came myself; they wanted to see *me*. Someone who had won an award for being the best tax expert for that year interrogated me. As I narrated my woes to this senior minister, he laughed and shook my hand. Surprised, I asked him why he was giving me a "pat on the back".

He answered, "Congratulations. I have filled that form five times. I have been through that process five different times." He went on to commend me, saying that I was maturing and paying the price to be in the high place of ministry. So you see, before you can occupy certain positions, you have to pay a price. When you pay the price, you enter the room that God has prepared for you.

Elisha Paid the Price for Elijah's Room

Elisha paid the price to take Elijah's room. When Elijah came to Elisha, he just threw his mantle on him. Elisha was surprised. He knew Elijah was calling him. Elijah himself was so sad about it. He knew that Elisha was going to make a great sacrifice.

"What have I done to you? What have I done?" Elijah asked.

Elisha told his business partners that he was quitting. He took his oxen and ended his business in one stroke. He divided up his business and walked away from it. He told himself, "It is over, I can't go back." He was going to follow Elijah. Elisha paid the price to stand in Elijah's room.

Joshua paid the price to take over from Moses. Peter, James and John paid the price to be apostles.

How many are going to live and sacrifice for Jesus? How many are going to stand in their rooms and pay the price? Get in there. God has a room for you. God had a room for me and I believe that He has one for you. I believe that there are more rooms to occupy and I intend to be there. You must determine to be in the room that God has for you!

F***urthermore, by these few pages, my son, be admonished because of making many books there is no end.***

CHAPTER 10

The Sacrifices of a Christian Leader

Then Peter began to say unto him, Lo, WE HAVE LEFT ALL, and have followed thee.

Mark 10:28

We see again the disciples having to sacrifice to follow Jesus. They left all! They left their professions, families and familiar friends to follow Jesus. It was a sacrifice. You cannot follow Jesus unless you are ready to sacrifice something.

Your ministry is limited by what you keep. If you carry certain things while you run, you will not run fast enough. God is expecting us to leave things behind on the altar and follow Him. We may have to leave our sleep, friendships, televisions, careers and jobs to follow Jesus.

There are pastors in large populated areas whose ministries do not grow because they are not prepared to lay down their lives.

The Sacrifice of Time

This is the most important sacrifice of a pastor. Without sacrificing time to be with the Lord, there will be no real fruit. Many ministers have time for everything else but the Lord. There is time for TV, socializing, computers, business and sports but there is no time for personal fellowship with the Lord. The ministry is a reflection of a man's personal time with the Lord.

The Sacrifice of Your Money

Many pastors do not know that they have to give their money to the ministry. I believe that every minister must invest personally into the ministry. Of course, you cannot do that if your money is not distinct from the church's money.

It is important that your personal possessions are distinct from the property of the church. If this distinction is not clear, you lose the blessing of giving. You have nothing to give because all you have is church property. And how can you give the church what belongs to it?

The Sacrifice of Your Comforts and Well- Being

There are many things in the ministry, which may take away your comforts. If you are not prepared to sacrifice the little things of life, you may never amount to much in the ministry.

Insisting on certain comforts on this earth can easily be the reason for your inability to progress in the ministry. You should "*set your affection on things above, not on things on the earth*" (Colossians 3:2). When your heart is set on things above, you will not be so fussy about things on this earth.

One night, I was standing by the Pacific Ocean in a foreign country. In front of me were several large expensive yachts belonging to millionaires. I turned to the Christians who were walking with me and said, "I would like to have my yacht in Heaven." One of them laughed at me and said, "Oh no, I want to have mine *here*."

This little conversation reflects two schools of thought in Christendom today. Most Christians want to have their comforts here, while a few want them in Heaven.

I do not drive the car that I would really like to drive. In fact, I have never driven the car I really prefer. I also know the nicest and best cars but I do what I do for the sake of the ministry.

> **But I have used none of these things: neither have I written these things, that it should be so done unto me: for it were better for me to die, than that any man should make my glorying void.**
>
> **1 Corinthians 9:15**

I do not live in the best house or in the best area of my city. I do know where these "best areas" and "best houses" are. I do know that there are many better places than where I live. I am also aware that my church can afford to provide these things for me. But I am content with what the Lord has given me. In fact, I think I am super blessed. I do not intend to join the struggle to impress people about what I have and where I live. I hope to have the best mansions in Heaven and not here on Earth.

The Sacrifice of Your Family

Your family will make many sacrifices because of the ministry. You will have to give up time and pleasure with your family so that you can do the work. In Luke 14, the young man refused to attend the dinner because he had "married a wife".

> **And another said, I HAVE MARRIED A WIFE, and therefore I cannot come.**
>
> **Luke 14:20**

Many people do not fulfil God's will because they try to please their wives. The Bible teaches us to love our wives. But the Bible teaches us to love God first.

> **If any man come to me, and hate not his father, and mother, and wife, and children, and brethren, and sisters, yea, and his own life also, he cannot be my disciple.**
>
> **Luke 14:26**

Jesus talks about hating your mother, your father, your wife, your children, your brethren, your sisters and even your own life in order to be a disciple. If you have to do that to qualify as a disciple, how much more would you have to do that as a Christian leader?

The Sacrifice of Your Safety and Security

Jesus sacrificed the safety of Heaven to dwell amongst a group of perverted, depraved and wicked people. We must follow His example if we are to bear fruit.

Walking with the Lord will lead you into many dangers, toils and snares. Every journey you make will put you at risk. If your self-preservation is more important than obeying God, you are not likely to sacrifice your safety and security.

Being in full-time ministry means you must sacrifice your security. It is much more secure to work for Barclays Bank than it is to work for a Pentecostal church led by a twenty-eight-year-old pastor.

I was once invited to Colombia to minister. I was uncertain as to whether I should go or not. I called a pastor in America to ask whether he knew if Colombia was a safe place to go to. He told me he would find out and call me back.

He called me a couple of days later and said, "Brother, it is a very dangerous place. I don't think you should venture there."

He continued, "I talked to a Catholic nun who told me to advice you not to step in Colombia. She told me of a

Catholic bishop who had been shot in cold blood while serving mass."

"Are you serious!" I exclaimed.

"Yes," he replied. "It is very dangerous."

Then, I had some further information. I was told about another pastor who had been shot while getting into his car after church. It became clear to me that pastors were a target in Colombia. I also remembered a renowned pastor who had almost died in a drive-by shooting incident in Bogotá.

Of course, I decided I would not set foot in Colombia. However, as I flew down to another country in South America, I had a dream in which the Lord spoke to me. He rebuked me sharply and told me that He was ashamed of me because I was trying to preserve myself. He reminded me that if He removed His protection from me for just five minutes, I would perish instantly. When I woke up, I was frightened and decided to go to Colombia. I needed no further coaxing to take me to Colombia.

Dear friend, I cannot begin to describe the extent of the power of God that was present in those meetings in Colombia. I saw the greatest miracles in my life, including the raising of the dead.

Furthermore, by these few pages, my son, be admonished because of making many books there is no end.

CHAPTER 11

Give it or Lose it

Therefore doth my Father love me, because I lay down my life, that I might take it again. No man taketh it from me, but I lay it down of myself. I have power to lay it down, and I have power to take it again. This commandment have I received of my Father.

John 10:17-18

Jesus was clever; He knew it was a matter of time before the Pharisees would kill Him. He knew that it was just a matter of time before He would be eliminated. The build up of hatred was obvious to all. *Instead of waiting for this to happen, He gave up Himself to be crucified.*

The Great Difference

There is a great difference between giving up something and having it taken from you. In both cases, you end up losing the thing. **To give something is a blessing but to**

lose something is a curse. I have watched as people tried to preserve themselves and their families but ended up losing them. Many have also tried to prevent financial loss as they avoided going into full-time ministry. Somehow, they lost what they were trying to keep.

I remember one lady who was trying to prevent the loss of her husband by keeping him away from the church. Anytime church members came to see her husband for some help, she would shoo them away. Her nasty and unwelcoming behaviour was a clear indication to the visitors that they were not wanted. Gradually, she warded away the church members until her vision of securing her husband to herself was accomplished. However, after sometime, her husband began to backslide. He no longer attended prayer meetings and became uninterested in church. As he became less spiritual, he also began to lose interest in his wife. Soon, his eyes were twinkling and his mouth was watering. He considered other girls.

This lady realized that she was about to lose what she was guarding. Then she ran to church and asked the pastor to pray for her marriage. The very thing she was preserving was slipping away.

Dear friend, be it known unto you that he who keeps his life will lose it and he who loses his life for Christ's sake will find it. These are the irrevocable words of our Saviour.

> **He that findeth his life shall lose it: and he that loseth his life for my sake shall find it.**

There are people who think they are preserving their family lives by not getting too involved in church activities. They give themselves to secular pursuits thinking that they are safeguarding the future of their homes. Many of these people have ended up losing their children and their spouses as they followed money on a wild goose chase.

Give it Before it Is Taken

A prudent man foreseeth the evil, and hideth himself: but the simple pass on, and are punished.

Proverbs 22:3

It takes wisdom to see ahead and to know that you are going to lose something. Foolishness often keeps us blinded from this reality.

I once ran a car rental business. At one point, I had a very good customer who was paying me good money. At times, he would rent my car for long periods and promise to pay later. This suited me fine until the payments stopped coming. After one or two months of waiting, I decided to go fetch my car. I eventually got the car but my customer would not pay up and kept telling me stories.

I made several trips to a suburb of Accra trying to get this man to pay. One night, the Lord told me that I was never going to get my money. He asked me to give the money to the man as a gift. (The Lord was introducing me to an eternal principle). I was going to lose something anyway so I might as well give it away first.

But I thought I was wiser than the Lord. The man had

been so insolent that I didn't feel like giving him anything. I decided to pursue this man until I got my money. My debtor was a smooth- talking liar, who had a different story each time.

Up till now, I have not gotten my money. I lost it. God knew I would lose it anyway. He wanted to bless me, so he asked me to take that step of giving it away but I failed to do so.

Give up your life or it will be taken from you.

Furthermore, by these few pages, my son, be admonished because of making many books there is no end.

CHAPTER 12

Sacrifice Brings the Glory

Thus all the work that Solomon made for the house of the LORD was finished: and Solomon brought in all the things that David his father had dedicated; and the silver, and the gold, and all the instruments, put he among the treasures of the house of God Then Solomon assembled the elders of Israel, and all the heads of the tribes, the chief of the fathers of the children of Israel, unto Jerusalem, to bring up the ark of the covenant of the LORD out of the city of David, which is Zion. Wherefore all the men of Israel assembled themselves unto the king in the feast which was in the seventh month. And all the elders of Israel came; and the Levites took up the ark. And they brought up the ark, and the tabernacle of the congregation, and all the holy vessels that were in the tabernacle, these did the priests and the Levites bring up. Also king

Solomon, and all the congregation of Israel that were assembled unto him before the ark, sacrificed sheep and oxen, which could not be told nor numbered for multitude. And the priests brought in the ark of the covenant of the LORD unto his place, to the oracle of the house, into the most holy place, even under the wings of the cherubims: For the cherubims spread forth their wings over the place of the ark, and the cherubims covered the ark and the staves thereof above. And they drew out the staves of the ark, that the ends of the staves were seen from the ark before the oracle; but they were not seen without. And there it is unto this day.

There was nothing in the ark save the two tables which Moses put therein at Horeb, when the LORD made a covenant with the children of Israel, when they came out of Egypt. And it came to pass, when the priests were come out of the holy place: (for all the priests that were present were sanctified, and did not then wait by course: Also the Levites which were the singers, all of them of Asaph, of Heman, of Jeduthun, with their sons and their brethren, being arrayed in white linen, having cymbals and psalteries and harps, stood at the east end of the altar, and with them an hundred and twenty priests sounding with trumpets:) It came even to pass, as the trumpeters and singers were as one, to make one sound to be heard in praising and thanking the LORD; and when they lifted up their voice with the trumpets and cymbals and instruments of musick, and praised the LORD, saying, For he is good; for his mercy endureth for ever: that then the house was filled with a cloud, even the house of the LORD; So that the

priests could not stand to minister by reason of the cloud: for the glory of the LORD had filled the house of God.

2 Chronicles 5:1-14

And the breasts and the right shoulder Aaron waved for a wave offering before the LORD; as Moses commanded. And Aaron lifted up his hand toward the people, and blessed them, and came down from offering of the sin offering, and the burnt offering, and peace offerings. And Moses and Aaron went into the tabernacle of the congregation, and came out, and blessed the people: and the glory of the LORD appeared unto all the people. And there came a fire out from before the LORD, and consumed upon the altar the burnt offering and the fat: which when all the people saw, they shouted, and fell on their faces.

Leviticus 9:21-24

As you can see in these accounts, when they offered sacrifice, the glory of God filled the temple. Do you want to see the glory of God in your life? Then do not shy away from the sacrifice that God has placed before you. A minister who has the glory of God on his life has often paid the price of sacrifice.

The Price of Glory Is the Same

I have noticed that there is no successful minister who does not have a story of suffering and difficulties.

Recently, a visiting minister, whose ministry I knew little about, came to speak in our church. As he shared his life testimony, I marvelled at how this principle is played out in everyone's life.

He had been through many things. He had gone hungry on many occasions; he had encouraged his wife on several occasions. He had been without money and food many times. This man is now a very successful minister in the country where he lives. The story is the same everywhere. There is a sacrifice behind the glory of God!

Solomon made many sacrifices to the Lord. Suddenly, the glory filled the temple and no one could stand to minister. God was moved by the sacrifice. God is still moved by your sacrifice.

> **And it was told king David, saying, The LORD hath blessed the house of Obed-edom, and all that pertaineth unto him, because of the ark of God. So David went and brought up the ark of God from the house of Obed-edom into the city of David with gladness. And it was so, that when they that bare the ark of the LORD had gone six paces, he sacrificed oxen and fatlings.**
>
> **2 Samuel 6:12-13**

This story shows us how King David made innumerable sacrifices as he brought in the ark of God. The ark of God represents the anointing. The ark represents the glory of God. After every six steps, they would sacrifice oxen and fatling. Can you imagine how many sacrifices they must have made from Obed-edom's house to the City of David? This journey of faith symbolizes the amount of sacrifice required to bring in the glory.

Furthermore, by these few pages, my son, be admonished because of making many books there is no end.

CHAPTER 13

Blessings on Earth, Blessings in Heaven

And Jesus answered and said, Verily I say unto you, There is no man that hath left house, or brethren, or sisters, or father, or mother, or wife, or children, or lands, for my sake, and the gospel's, BUT HE SHALL RECEIVE AN HUNDREDFOLD now in this time, houses, and brethren, and sisters, and mothers, and children, and lands, with persecutions; and in the world to come eternal life.
Mark 10:29-30

God promises that we shall receive a hundredfold blessing now and in the world to come. You can be blessed on Earth as you serve the Lord. God is an all-rounder. It is time to believe in His glory. We must believe that He is a rewarder of them that diligently seek Him (Hebrews 11:6).

Expect rewards as you serve the Lord. Expect them on Earth and in Heaven.

I have been surprised by the Lord. I honestly thought that I was going to be poor and wretched as I followed the road of ministry. I thought I would never have anything. To my surprise, God has given me a hundredfold in this life. How true the Scriptures can be. He that loses his life will save it and he that saves it, will lose it.

> **He that findeth his life shall lose it: and he that loseth his life for my sake shall find it.**
>
> **Matthew 10:39**

Because of this Gospel I have travelled all over the world. There were times I was treated as royalty and I wondered who was making a mistake.

Are you afraid to trust the Lord? You are making the greatest mistake of your life. Give yourself to Him. It is worth the risk! It is worth it! There is a hymn, by George Bennard, that blesses my heart. It speaks about the cross of Christ. As you read through the words, may the Lord inspire you to lay down your life for Him!

The Old Rugged Cross

On a hill far away, stood an old rugged cross

The emblem of suffering and shame,
And I love that old cross

Where the dearest and best, for a world
of lost sinners was slain

Oh that old rugged cross, So despised by the world
Holds a wondrous attraction to me,
For t'was on that old cross
Jesus suffered and died, To pardon and sanctify me
To the old rugged cross, I will ever be true
It's shame and reproach gladly bear, Then He'll call me some day
To my home far away, Where His glory forever I'll share.

Chorus

So I'll cherish the old rugged cross, Till my trophies at last I'll lay down
I will cling to the old rugged cross, and exchange it some day for a crown.

Furthermore, by these few pages, my son, be admonished because of making many books there is no end.

Other Books by Dag Heward-Mills

Mini Size Books

Beauty

Duality

Frugality

Born Again

Fornication

The Secret

The Tent Ministry

They Went To Hell

7 Great Principles

Solomonic Success

The Strange Woman

Secrets Of Success

Supernatural Power

Principles Of Success

100% Answered Prayer

Strategies For Prayer

Unbeatable Prosperity

How To Start A Church

Forgiveness Made Easy

Sacrifice Versus Obedience

Preaching Teaching Healing

Poison - Taming Your Tongue

Key Facts For New Christians

Anagkazo - Compelling Power

Bearing Fruit After Your Own Kind

How To Recognise Demons At Work

How To Overcome Barrenness In Ministry

Opportunities (Previously Titled As Prodigality)

Proton

Success and wealth

My Father, my father

The words of Jesus

Take up your Cross

Leadership Books

How To Become A Leader

The Successful Leader

Essentials Of Leadership

Principles Of Leadership

Aids To Leadership

Wisdom For Leaders

Excellence In Leadership

Leading Difficult People

Leadership Made Easy

Lecture Notes On Leadership

Devotional Books

Your Daily Quiet Time

Standard Size Books

Win The Lost

Art Of Hearing

Ministerial Ethics

Catch The Anointing

Full Size Books (Soft-back)

Quiet Time

Backsliding

Mega Church

Church Planting

Name It Claim It Take It

Loyalty And Disloyalty

Lay People And Ministry

Transform Your Pastoral Ministry

Hard Back Books

Quiet Time

Church Planting

Leaders And Loyalty

Ministers Hand Book

The Art Of Leadership

Loyalty And Disloyalty

Transform Your Pastoral Ministry

For additional information on Dag Heward-Mills' books, audio tapes, CDs and videos write to:

In Africa:
Parchment House
P. O. Box DC 1034
Dansoman
Accra, Ghana
West Africa

The Rest of the world:
Lighthouse Chapel International
P. O. Box 3706
London
NW2 1YJ
United Kingdom

or visit

Website:

www.daghewardmills.org